SWEET ASTRID

Amy Neal

Sweet Astrid

©2021, Amy Neal

www.nealamy.com

ISBN: 978-1-09838-738-9
ISBN eBook: 978-1-09838-739-6

To my hermosa hermana,
I love your guts, Gut

You don't have to believe in God
but please collapse in wonder
as regularly as you can

try and let your knowledge
be side swiped by awe
and let beauty be so persuasive
you find yourself willing
to lay your opinions at her feet

Darling, you don't have to believe in God
but please pray for your own sake
great prayers of thanks
for the mountains, the great rivers
the roundness of the moon
just because they're here at all
and that you get to know them
and let prayer bubble up in you
as a natural thing
like song in a bird

You don't have to have
a spiritual path but do run
the most sensitive
part of your soul
over the soft curves
of this world
with as much tenderness
as you can find in yourself
and let her edgeless ways
inspire you to discover more

just find a way
that makes you want to yield
yourself
that you may be more open
to letting beauty fully
into your arms

and feel some sacred flame
inside of you that yearns toward
learning how to build a bigger
fire of love in your heart

You don't have to believe in God
but get quiet enough to remember
we really don't know a damn thing
about any of it
and if you can, feel a reverence to be part
of This Great Something
whatever you want to call it
that is so much bigger
and so far beyond the rooftops of all
our knowing

—Chelan Harkin, Susceptible to Light

TABLE OF CONTENTS

FOUR, ACTUALLY

England, 2009

The first time I went to England I visited Buckingham Palace. What I mean to say is that I *actually went inside* Buckingham Palace. Dave won an award.

Stick with me for a minute while I blow my husband's trumpet: Dave was in the Royal Navy for 27 years, and just after retirement, he was awarded an OBE (an Officer in the Order of the British Empire) by The Royal Family. It was a tremendous honour for Dave and, by extension, our family. Dave's parents were in their eighties, and they attended the ceremony at the palace with us.

My recollection of that day, over a decade ago now, is a blurry one. The memories come to me like isolated jewels, popping forth from the gossamer setting of the past. I remember we took my first and only classic London taxi. In my stomach, excited butterflies battled against waves of nausea as I faced backward on the twisting, stop-and-go journey from the train station at Charing Cross to the palace gates. Across from me sat Dave's parents, Danny and Pam, his father and stepmum of 25 years. To me, Dave's parents represented a golden age in their country. Like in Narnia, they, too, had been children during WW2, and they'd reached life's milestones in matching step with their Queen. Danny and Pam were hard-working, well-mannered, middle-class Londoners who'd taken the train to work in the city for 40 years. They were my introduction to England—the sort of couple who dressed up before going to the "greengrocer's" in the high street, and the type who served gin and tonics in Pam's glorious garden on rare sunny days. Danny and Pam made a place for me at the family table, and they were kind. In the black cab that day, we were on our way to see royalty, but Dave and I were accompanied by pure class.

Inside the palace, as we made our way to the room for the ceremony, I remember a pristine suit of armor—utterly flawless and gleaming silver, there was not a single indentation or smudge on the obviously hollow, life-size soldier. And yet, I still felt wary as if the Queen's glorious protector might not let me pass.

Pam and I both needed the loo, so we asked an attendant where to spend-a-penny before the ceremony started. Inside the restroom was an enormous, antique toilet with a complex chain flush. It was the size of an American clothes dryer. I remember being disconcerted as I climbed aboard the potty and rearranged my finest clothing. Then, I did my business into a great historic box of foreign gadgetry. The experience was surreal and unnerving, too much like waking up from a dream, horrified to find I'd tinkled in my bed.

Back in the presentation room, we made our way to our seats. Pam had a degenerative eye disease and was legally blind, although she still had some peripheral vision. "Stiff upper lip" and all, Pam made due for familiar bus trips to the grocery store, but otherwise she was largely homebound. At 82, she had been putting off getting a walking stick for the blind, but she ordered one especially for our day at the palace. Months earlier, when the royal invitation arrived, our family was pleased when she finally agreed to tick the box for preferential seating due to medical reasons. I think Pam felt she needed that stick to justify the tick. So, on our day at the palace, while Dave and the other awardees were ushered into an adjoining room, I escorted my elderly in-laws up to our seats on the very front row––an ignorant young American leading the blind.

Meanwhile, in the side room, Dave was talked through a series of royal protocols and ceremonial procedures, which he later shared with me. Essentially, it had to do with queueing up, bows, and curtsies. Awardees were to enter the room, one by one, from stage left. Dave would be primed when the proceeding person's name was called so he needed to be ready. Then, by the time his name was announced, Dave should be positioned to: 1) Step forward, 2) Turn left and bow at the prince from 10 feet away, 3) Walk forward to stand directly in front of the prince, 4) Bow again, 5) DO NOT TOUCH HIS ROYAL HIGHNESS or try to shake his hand, 6) Have a little chat and get a prize, 7) Bow again, 8) Walk backward six steps, 9) Bow again, 10) Turn and exit stage right. Given the excitement of the day, it was a lot to remember—I imagine a bit like having to learn a dance five minutes before performing it (to a room full of strangers and a prince, whose lineage had a history of beheading people.)

I remember being incredibly impressed when the ceremony started *precisely* on time, to the very second, according to the clock on the wall. As the royal entourage entered the room, I was surprised and dazzled by the two, fierce-looking Asian soldiers in distinctive, crisp green uniforms with curved knives. Dave later told me these men were Gurkhas from Nepal, known as the "The Bravest of the Brave." In time, I'd come to learn that out of 10,000

Nepalese applicants, approximately only 240 soldiers were selected for the British Army's Brigade of Gurkhas. And, of that elite brigade, the two men before me had been selected to protect the heir to the throne. Even at the time, without the cultural background, I could tell those royal guards were guys with whom one should not fuck.

In all the fanfare, I had missed an important gentleman in the middle. When I finally recognized Prince Charles, His Royal Highness, The Prince of Wales, I felt disbelief. It was difficult to reconcile this unassuming human before me, a man my father's age, to that "future King of England" I'd seen on TV. As he settled into position up front, I fought my urge to charge the stage, to cackle and tackle the Prince. Instead, I captured and held him with my eyes, and as the morning unfolded, I realized something significant about the man. Believe it or not, for better or worse, Charles was a real person—an actual human being. Imperfect? Absolutely. Not unlike me.

I think hundreds of people received an award that day, with numbers diminishing in proportion to the prestige of the title being awarded. To my recollection, only one or two people were knighted, the top honour of the day. It was all a blur.

I remember nerves were running high since it was one of the most notable days in many attendees' lives. It was endearing and comical and vicariously embarrassing to watch Britain's best and brightest bungle it all up. *I was rooting for them all!* Yet, some forgot to step forward when the proceeding person's name was called. Several overlooked one of the four bows. One guy tried to shake the Prince's hand—to which His Royal Highness smiled kindly and gently redirected. Another lady received her medal and excitedly turned her back to the Prince, forgetting both to curtsy and to back away and curtsy. She remembered several steps too late and, *mortified*, lurched awkwardly back to triple-curtsy away any unintended insult. Bless their hearts; I felt for them. But folks, between us, it was a bit of a dog's dinner. And through it all, Prince Charles was generous and gracious.

When Dave's name was called, though, my husband nailed it. He looked completely at ease like he'd done this dance a thousand times before. When he got to the Prince, Dave later told me they shared a few quick words about flying. It seemed the gentlemen had something in common.

I should probably back up to explain an OBE, an Officer in the Order of the British Empire, because most American's have no idea what that means. An "O. B. E." is a level two out of five, with level five being a knighthood—the ones who, still to this day, get the sword tapped on their shoulders. Those knighted can add the title "Sir" or "Dame" to the front of their name. Twice a year, the Royal Family honours top citizens in civil and military divisions for their outstanding work in the fields of arts, sciences, charity, welfare, and national defense. Dave was chosen for his work in The Joint Strike Fighter Program, to help build the next great military jet. To most Britons, to be granted a place in the chivalric Order of the British Empire would be an honour (although there are those who are *not* enamored by or supportive of the monarchy). To our family, it was a big dang deal.

Technically, only knights can be entitled "Sir" or "Dame." However, that OBE is how Dave earned his nickname "Sir." Mind you, when I call my husband "Sir," it isn't from a place of deference. Me calling Dave "Sir" is a bit like Marcy talking to Peppermint Patty in the *Peanuts* cartoon *(except that Dave is Charlie Brown, and I'm Peppermint Patty)*. Or, it would be like naming your family dog "Duke." Regardless, having procured a good marriage, my station in life was elevated, and Dave anointed me "Madam." To this day, we still call each other by our titles, even in our pajamas.

After the ceremony, we had our photos taken as a family in the courtyard. Today, as I write, I am looking across to a bookshelf with a photograph of the four of us smiling back at me. In the photo, Danny's face is bursting with pride for his son. I have no doubt that Dave's mother Lorna, who passed away from cancer when Dave was 18, would have been incredibly proud, too.

When it was all said and done, I took delight in imagining our family to be quite scandalous, a source of juicy gossip for "the royal court," like in all those British television programs I'd seen. I pictured women's heads together, a tangling of malicious whispers and those bizarre hair decorations called "fascinators." First, they'd see Pam, a matron who was obviously angling for preferential treatment as she tapped around with that prop cane of hers— *More like a blind percussionist!* they'd titter. Then, they'd zero in on me, Dave's too-young, American, participation trophy wife. *Can you believe she got a free pass into Buckingham Palace on her first trip to England? There are thousands of hardworking, loyal British subjects more deserving of the honour. I hear she even sat in the front row. I bet that trollop is a drain on the National Health Service, too!*

In all seriousness, the event at the palace was a highlight in all four of our lives. We were so proud of Dave on that magical day, and, for a time, we all lived happily ever after. We couldn't know then, that five years later both Danny and Pam would pass away. My time with my in-laws felt far too short. However, even without that special trip to Buckingham Palace, Danny and Pam had shown me the very best of England.

During that initial trip to England, I met one of Dave's childhood friends for the first time, too. One evening Simon said to me, "You sound just like that actress from *What's Eating Gilbert Grape!*"

I beg your pardon, I thought, unsure if I should be insulted.

We all spoke English, but clearly something had gotten lost in translation.

Let me interpret: Juliette Lewis was a phenomenal young actor, and starting in my teenage years I was drawn to her work because she was only three years older than me. She was incredibly talented and in several amazing, top movies. To my memory at the time, however, let's just say she wasn't known for playing the sharp crayons in the box. Her first major role, for example, was the ditsy teenaged daughter Audrey Griswold in the slapstick comedy *National Lampoon's Christmas Vacation*. In the early nineties, Ms. Lewis went on to choose delicious, dark films with complicated characters in which she portrayed a variety of southern, slow-witted, troubled young women, those that were often a little bit on the trashy side (bless their hearts). Her ignorant characters made terrible life choices in films like *Cape Fear*, *Natural Born Killers*, and *Kalifornia*.

So, when Simon connected our accents, I immediately pictured Ms. Lewis in the movie *Kalifornia* where she's flashing one breast to entice her serial killer boyfriend (played by) Brad Pitt back into their mobile home.

"I'll be waiting for you when you get back," she drawls.

"Put yer titty back up, Adele /A-dell/," he twangs.

And *that's* the Juliette Lewis I knew, loved, and remembered when Simon said we seemed alike.

I've since re-watched Lasse Hallström's incredible film *What's Eating Gilbert Grape* (1993), and to credit Simon's ear, Juliette sounded a lot less *countrified* in it than she did in *Kalifornia* (Dominic Sena, 1993). Still, she lived in a trailer. Even at the time, I wanted to believe my husband's friend meant no offense, and that as an Englishman, surely he didn't recognize the cultural implications. Simon was (and is) a fine chap—a kindhearted person, truly. However, when Simon said I sounded like that slow southern character, it probably felt similar to an American telling a British woman that she reminded them of a reality television star from that show *The Only Way is Essex*.

Oh. I see. How remarkable. Feck you very much, indeed.

In all fairness, I've had a chip on my shoulder about my intelligence since I was nine years old. Growing up, my older sister Julie (who happens to be Juliette's age) was in the "gifted and talented" program at school. She *passed* an intelligence test in 3rd grade (Year 4), which qualified her for extension lessons. Once a day, she and all the other smart kids were paraded (with little noses raised high in the air) down the hall before disappearing for an hour or two into the mysterious P.E.A.K. classroom. In that secret chamber, their otherwise bored minds were stimulated with puzzles, projects, and a bunch of extra work (or so my sister tells me). I can't recall what P.E.A.K. stood for, but I think it was something like Petty Exceptionally Arrogant Kids. I couldn't wait to join their exclusive ranks.

Four years later, when my turn rolled around, I can remember being pulled into the school counselor's office to take the P.E.A.K. test. I started off overconfident like most bright kids, but as the test increased in difficulty I started to crack up, especially on the timed puzzles. Anxiety began to course through my shaking little body as I realized my reputation was on the line. Alas, I panicked and shut down. After the whole episode, I, the dumber sister, was found to be neither gifted nor talented, let alone smart enough to be in P.E.A.K. I *failed* the IQ test. Instead of extension lessons, convincing myself that I was worthwhile and smart became my own fun little side project, some extra work for my otherwise "high-(but)-average" mind.

Years later, as often happens in stories like these, I turned to the dark arts. To exact my evil retribution, I decided to certify as an educational diag-nostician to, you know, shatter the souls of children. As a part of that Master's degree, I would qualify to give intelligence tests to students, and, therefore, I needed to give practice IQ tests to several people. So, as one does, I roped in my husband.

For years I'd covertly assumed Dave was pretty smart, given that he had that OBE and was selected out of hundreds, perhaps thousands, of people to fly bazillion-dollar jets and all that *(despite being a terrible driver)*. Naturally, I kept my suspicions of Dave's high intellect inside—mostly as a service to others, to keep the man tolerable. It was no surprise to me when he did well on my examiner's practice test, but I was disgruntled to see that he scored in the tippy-top percentages of all intelligence areas. *Bugger!* Dave seemed to think afterward that his results should, for once and for all, prove to me that he was, what we Americans call, "one-smart-cookie." I, however, reminded Dave that I was merely an unqualified student-examiner who had no doubt made several mistakes during the test administration. He wasn't buying it.

To make matters worse, later that same year Dave finished his degree in Developmental Economics with the London School of Economics (despite, *rather flakily*, going on to be a high school physics teacher instead*)*. Upon completion of the course, he received a letter saying that he had the highest exam scores of any student in the program that year.

He didn't even gloat, which was worse. In truth, Dave had always been a humble and patient man while I was the one more prone to trash-talking and meltdowns (a bit like playing Monopoly with an eight-year-old). However, I've got to say, that valedictorian letter broke me. After that, how could I not acknowledge his ample brains? Despite being a more substantial meal, of the two of us, Dave was clearly more likely to be the long-term survivor of a zombie apocalypse.

Faced with Dave's undeniably greater intelligence, I was reminded of an educational theory that teachers sometimes used to sort kids into classrooms. It worked like this: Every child in 3rd grade (for example) was assigned a ranking from one to five, with "one" for students that struggled the most significantly in school and "five" for the most successful students. It was based on a Bell curve, so the majority of kids ended up being Twos, Threes, and Fours, and very few kids were Ones or Fives.

Without gouging too deeply into how the theory worked, for fear one might pop out an eyeball, just know that Fours couldn't be placed in the same classroom as Fives because Fours were *juuust* bright enough to get lazy. Fours were the kids in group projects who sat back and let the Fives do all the work. Over time, Fours often quit trying when paired with more confident, *know-it-all* Fives since those kids tended to get answers a second or two more quickly. However, put a Four with a Three, Two, or One and they'd likely rise to leadership. Well, in theory anyway.

What do I know? I'm just a Four, married to a fuckin' Five.

Through the years, evidence of my intelligence has often been serendipitous, a bit like a white-privileged version of the movie *Slumdog Millionaire*. For example, the last time I played Trivial Pursuit with my British family, I managed to earn my team a blue cheese when asked,

"Lake Tana in the northern highlands of Ethiopia is the source of what river?"

The Blue Nile. *Duh.* The only reason I knew the answer was because I'd lived in Ethiopia for three years and I had taken a sightseeing tour on the lake.

A similar experience once happened with my parents in Texas while watching the game show *Jeopardy*. I was able to correctly rattle off the answers to all five questions about Asian languages *(including the Daily Double!),* and only because I'd spent almost a decade in the East, South East, and South regions of the continent. The questions weren't linguistically difficult. For example, they asked to identify various scripts and simple greetings, or contestants were asked how to say "Thank You" in Korean. The quizzing did cover a range of Asian countries. After my winning streak, my parents were very impressed, and both turned to stare at me, "Ol' Confucius" on their couch. I was pretty shocked, too. I may be a world traveler, but let's face it—I'm more of a roly-poly than I am a polyglot.

I love visiting England, but I find it surprisingly challenging sometimes, especially in those earlier years, before I was bilingual. There is so much that gets lost in the Atlantic Ocean.

For example, take the phrase "fast train to Charing Cross—calling in Waterloo." It totally stumped me at first. *Aren't all trains fast? I mean, surely all trains go at least 45 mph. And what do they mean by "calling?" Like, telephoning? Are the trains planning to phone their grandmas, like in the show* Thomas the Train?

"Hello, Gran."

"Oh hello, poppet!"

"Gran! Guess what! I'm carrying a load of Turkish delight today!"

"Turkish Delight! Oh, Thomas, how delightful!"

Wait? Was that my stop? WE DIDN'T STOP!

In England, I always understand the actual words being said, but sometimes I can't put them together to make sense—well, at least not quickly, and certainly not at London speeds.

My incredibly quick British family can compound my distress, with their five Master's degrees, two Ph.Ds, one Cambridge "Pure Maths" graduate, four educators, two contemporary dancers (including performances at the reknowed theatre Sadler's Wells), and all of them being world travellers. No, Dave's sister Gwendolyn and her husband John don't live in a shoe with ten children. They're a family of five (plus a squishy-wishy new generation). Anyway, talk about "gifted and talented."

It can be difficult to hold my own as an American Four in a family of British Fives. During the Christmas holidays, for example, we love to solve puzzles and play games together, but I often end up feeling mildly (and sometimes significantly) dimwitted. Part of the trouble for me is cultural. The games we play are produced in Great Britain so they include regionally slanted quiz questions with obscure answers like: Macbeth, Arsenal (evidently, a men's soccer team), and Northern Ireland (definitely not "*Southern* Ireland," I'm told).

I've also been introduced to "cryptic" crossword puzzles. These very British word games are similar to regular crossword puzzles, except that instead of feeling simply stuck, an American can experience what it feels like to be an actual Beagle. Try this clue, for example:

1 – Across - (5 letters): Right to leave the body in the thicket

I'm led to believe it's not rocket science. Dave assures me that the answer to this question is straightforward, an easy one that most any Brit of average intelligence will get. (I'll even write the answer and an explanation at the end of this essay, but prepare your fuzzy hearts because it won't help one lick.)

Meanwhile, while doing a basic crossword puzzle with my uncharacteristically perplexed English family I was able to provide the answer to this question:

1 – Across – (6 letters): A classic American campfire snack with graham crackers, chocolate, and a marshmallow

Yep. I sure earned my Christmas dinner that year.

On a side note, for those of you sitting back, chuckling patiently at me and the rest of us nincompoops, let me take a moment to remind you of the Dunning-Kruger Effect, based on studies done by Justin Kruger and David Dunning from Cornell University. Wikipedia, a questionable, albeit quick, go-to resource for people like me, defines the Dunning-Kruger Effect as, "a cognitive bias in which people with low ability at a task overestimate their ability. It is related to the cognitive bias of illusory superiority and comes from the inability of people to recognize their lack of ability."

Are you sure you're a Five, Einstein?

Of course, it doesn't help that I lack that enviable, charming British skill to make witty, interesting chit-chat. I'm a terrible dinner guest, and I struggle with social anxiety. It's not a *diagnosed* medical condition, just a bloody unfortunate one. I'll sit awkwardly, accidentally scowling while inwardly thinking, *What should I say? Oh God, what should I say? Come on, Amy! Just say something!* At times like these, it rarely goes well because I end up over-compensating. I'll paste on a forced, vapid smile, and then I find myself (God help us) "acting American." I can't explain why that feels expected of me, or what it's even supposed to look like, and yet, for the life of me, I can't seem to disappoint. I manage to work expressions like "Cowabunga, Dude!" and "fanny pack" into conversations, which pop from my mouth without my consent. (I'm from Texas, not California, a state I've only visited twice. On neither occasion did I go surfing nor did I enjoy hands-free rollerblading along a boardwalk.) Folks, the overall effect certainly doesn't help my IQ appearance. Neither does the fact that, at times like these, I have been known to drink. A lot.

Just when one thinks it cannot possibly get worse for this Yank at a British dinner party, someone will inevitably bring up American politics. Imagine. Is it a surprise to learn the subject isn't my strong suit?

Y'all, my primary problems with talkin' politics have been the following: A) I can see both sides of almost any issue, B) I often don't know what I feel about a subject (until I write about it), and C) I'd much rather we all laugh and get along.

To further complicate political discussions abroad, the self-flagellating diplomat in me feels obligated to represent my entire country in a fair way, especially since our nation is so polarized. So while I lean Green and vote Blue, I recognize that most of my southern American family disagrees. For example, I support gun regulation. However, I've found myself in conversations where I end up explaining the values of my American brother-in-law whose gun collection rivals Osama bin Laden's. Overseas, I feel duty-bound to illustrate that many Americans have opposing views, as well as to express my own, often underdeveloped, positions. Basically, I end up explaining *how* many Americans think, rather than what I think, and in trying to be impartial, I sometimes end up sounding uncertain and hazy—like a weak, high-pitched fart, bubbling forth from someplace near the treacle pudding.

However, even in my 40s, I'm still learning and evolving. In recent years, I've come to see that me poo-pooing politics is a perk of my privilege because I haven't spent my life fighting to be seen, heard, or valued. So, I'm trying to do better, Folks—to engage and to use my voice for social justice.

In fact, there was a chapter, not too long ago, when I found it impossible to be neutral when I talked about American politics. When the topic came up, I was so filled with outrage that I both worried and hoped that I would catch fire and burn, burn, BURN! I wasn't always diplomatic, but I still tried to find unifying commonalities. For example, regardless of your nationality or political stance, I think all of us can agree on this: An *alarming* percentage of Americans are absolute morons.

And yet, teasing aside, we're all real people. Most of us aren't dumb enough make the news. My fellow Americans, we have to find ways to come together and heal—to recognize and respect the basic human dignity in each other. Heck, even this Four can see that.

So in closing, please don't doubt my high regard for Great Britain, Ireland, and the United States, as well as my appreciation for the fabulous Fives of the world. I mean, really, where would we be without those clever mofos? Also, please know that I have *fundamental respect* for (1) my diverse and nuanced family members (whom I care about through misunderstandings and even when we vehemently disagree), (2) Juliette Lewis, (3) the good people of Essex, (4) anyone who lives, or formerly lived, in a trailer park, (5) Arsenal fans, (6) those with a real knighthood, (7) Beagles, and (7) roly-polies. *(If there is anyone else I may have offended in the writing of this piece or in the book that follows, I encourage you to take out your typewriters and clackity-clack a letter of complaint to: His Royal Highness, The Prince of Wales, at Buckingham Palace with whom—as I believe you may already know, ahem—I have a personal connection.)*

Also, trust in the affection and pride I feel for my thick-skinned, big-brained husband, and, lastly, know that you don't need to fuss over me, quirky little Amy with her low self-esteem. Don't worry. I'm *juuust* bright enough to call "Shotgun." Besides, when we're not fighting for human rights, the fact is that many of us could benefit from taking ourselves a little less seriously. I don't mind being the butt of jokes I make about myself (as long as you are laughing with me, not at me, because you've learned how to laugh at yourself.). Still, consider this a warning: I'll pitch a hissy fit if *you* take the mickey out of *me*.

I will admit that living with an intellectually superior British husband can be both aggravating and humbling, but fear not. I keep him from getting too big for his britches. And, I'll let you in on a little secret: Deep down, in my own way, I suspect I'm a pretty sharp biscuit, too.

Take heart, America. I'm fixin' to make y'all proud! But listen, I'm gonna need sum' body to hold my beer, right quick, 'cause, first, I gotta put my titty back up.

Cryptic Crossword Question: (5 letters): Right to leave the body in the thicket

Cryptic Crossword Answer: Copse. Here's why: A word for "the body" is "corpse." When "right," which can be abbreviated to (R), leaves the word "corpse", you are left with "copse." *See what I mean, Snoopy?*

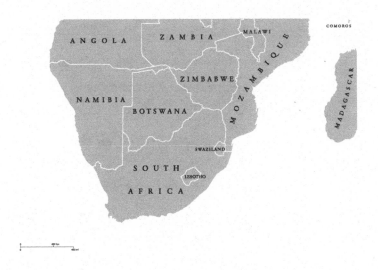

MOTHERLAND

Southern Africa, 2017

Western South Africa

"We could tell you weren't South African because you didn't have a *braai* last night. And today, when I saw that your *bakkie* was hired, we decided to ask you over for a *dop*," Ernie said, raising his feral eyebrows along with an empty plastic wine glass.

Ernie and Elmian, white South Africans in their early 60s, were also camping at the Witsand Nature Reserve on the edge of the Kalahari Desert. Ernie had introduced himself to me in the scullery as I washed up our dishes. He'd invited our family over to their campsite for an after-dinner drink.

"What's a 'bakkie?'" I asked.

"Oh, your truck. I think you call it a 'truck.'"

He pointed in the direction of our rented, 4X4, tent topped pickup.

"Here in South Africa, we call that a 'bakkie.'"

My husband Dave, Dave's 28-year-old daughter Paige, and I settled into our camp chairs around the fire, as Elmian poured us each a small glass of White Muscadel, an incredibly sweet South African wine. Sausages sizzled as Ernie flipped a handheld wire grill over the wood coals, and we sipped our liquid candy.

"So, my Bru, what brings you to South Africa?" Ernie opened.

"Well, we're here for two months on a road trip," Dave replied.

The couple seemed genuinely impressed and interested. They 'wow-ed!' and 'really-ed?' in all the right places, pulling the details out of us like a package of party streamers. Since we were showing off just a little, it wasn't hard to do.

Our trip started in South Africa. From there we would drive the bakkie, now dubbed "Bucky" in my mind, through Namibia, Botswana, Zimbabwe, Swaziland, Lesotho, and back into South Africa. After the road trip, we'd fly north to hike Mount Kenya, and then relax on the island of Zanzibar in Tanzania. Eight countries. The African portion of our "Midlife Gap Year" would take two full months. Teachers on a year's sabbatical, Dave and I had planned and saved for almost a decade to make it all happen. Dave's daughter Paige would join us for the first leg of our trip, and his sister Gwen would meet up with the family, later in our travels.

"Fantastic!" Elmian remarked and smiled brightly at me.

The two took a moment in Afrikaans to clarify something we'd said, but overall they understood quite well. Compared to Elmian, Ernie had more confidence speaking English, but I could tell he was the talker in either language.

"It sounds like you have a lekker trip planned. But, bladdy hell, did I hear you say that you're planning to drive through Zimbabwe, too?" he said.

Ernie let out a long whistle.

"Yes. Why? Is it dangerous?" Dave stammered.

"Ag no, nothing like that. You'll be safe, but it can be a bit tricky to get through the police roadblocks."

Ernie explained that police corruption could be a problem, and he gave us some tips for getting through the checkpoints. He said we'd be fine, but I wasn't so sure. I decided that, as a traveler with a year off work, I probably needed *something* to dread so I packed that worry away to suck on later.

That evening unfolded into one of the best of our entire trip. Elmian and Ernie were eager to make sure our stay in the region went as smoothly as possible, and they shaped our whole experience for the better. We discussed travel through southern Africa in general, and what to expect as we moved forward into Namibia, Botswana, and Zimbabwe. They answered all sorts of questions to the best of their knowledge, including those about the local tribes and the legendary tracking skill of Bushmen.

A true credit to a nation of carnivores, Ernie and Elmian introduced us to the art of the South African Braai. We got a crash course in barbequing, and the lessons included a sampling of gourmet sausages. Ernie talked us through which cuts of meat to buy from the local butchery, and Elmian wrote out a list for us in Afrikaans. We novices were assured that "Chili Beef Aromat" would be the only braai seasoning ever required, and they warned us not to gather firewood because some types were poisonous. They even drew us a map of the next town, which showed us where to buy the best biltong, and they gave us a sample. It tasted like jerky from Heaven (*Well, I mean, not Antelope Heaven*). As Ernie talked us through the map, it delighted me to learn that South Africans call traffic lights "robots," as in "turn left at the second robot."

All the while, Paige sat quietly at the edge of the firelight, feeding bits of boerewors to increasingly brave, little, striped wildcats. In the distance, southern stars and howling jackals reminded us how far we were from home. But, there at Ernie and Elmian's campfire, two generous locals made us feel warm and welcome. Our family was so fortunate to meet this lovely couple on the third night of our African adventure.

I had confidence that I was a reasonably bright woman, and I also understood that there were different types of intelligences. I knew that while I would probably score reasonably well on a test for English literacy, my scores for mechanical or technological problem-solving would likely rate me just slightly above, say, a chimpanzee. For example, I struggled to record a program on television using multiple remote controls or to adjust the defroster in a speeding, fogging rental car. Often what started with grunts and button smashing could quickly escalate into screams, fangs, and me throwing feces.

"What don't you understand?" Dave might ask in his superior British accent. "Just pull that lee-va!"

"I am pulling *the God-forsaken lee-va!*" I'd use my big girl words to explain.

Given my aptitude profile, living in the bakkie Bucky for a month was a challenge for me.

Bucky was a 4X4, white, crew cab Toyota Hilux, fully furnished for camping needs and topped with two tents. Designed for overlanding, the back of the truck was covered with a silver metal hardtop and underneath held everything a group of four would need to be self-sufficient, minus a shower or toilet.

Standing at either side of the vehicle, a person with average mechanical intelligence simply had to unlock and flip up a long metal hatch that ran the length of the truck bed. Inside was a camping kitchen furnished with aluminum sets of four—water cups, coffee cups, plates, bowls, and cutlery. Plus, there were basic cooking pots, a braai grid, a skillet, sharp knives, a teakettle, and a medium-sized flip-top refrigerator. It included two large butane gas cylinders, topped with stove burners, and a huge refillable water tank. There was even a table and camping chairs. Everything had its own little place and was secured down with bungee cords or by more complicated means.

The back door of the bakkie swung wide open on a side hinge to allow access to the cubbies. On a system of tracks, a person could pull out an enormous drawer, the width of the truck, which housed twelve to fifteen smaller compartments. A few of these were already filled with safety essentials like emergency triangles, a toolkit, and a puncture repair kit. However, most of these boxes would end up storing our food.

It being southern Africa, the truck was a right-side drive, a skill that was natural to my English family members and second nature to me, an American, by this point in life. With high ground clearance, 4WD, and two spare tires, the vehicle was perfect for our on-and-off-road journeys.

Basically, Bucky was badass, but first I had to learn to work everything.

We wasted no time finding our first African safari. After we left Ernie and Elmian, we headed north into the Kgalagardi Transfrontier Park, in the southern Kalahari Desert. Straddling the borders of South Africa and Botswana, and butting against Namibia, the park was an arid backdrop of red sand dunes, sparse vegetation, scattered trees, and dry riverbeds.

The wildlife was abundant. The park was home to a circle of life—where lions, cheetahs, leopards, and hyenas preyed on wildebeest, springbok, eland, and hartebeest. Enterprising vultures, raptors, buzzards, and secretary birds could be found dotting the skies and plains.

We approached the park in the late afternoon.

"So, do we just camp anywhere?" I asked apprehensively, pinning myself as the slowest, juiciest morsel in our party.

"Oh no. Don't worry," Dave clarified. "We'll be staying in a fenced campground at the edge of the park. They actually close the gates at sunrise and sunset. But tonight, I've booked us a night safari."

At camp we popped our tents up and situated ourselves for the evening. By this time, almost a week into our travels, we'd worked the kinks out in our routine. I'd gotten pretty good at removing the ratchets and climbing up to stand on the wheels to take off the tent covers, but putting those suckers back on would never be easy. The tents rose manually, using the ladder as leverage. Setting up camp was much faster than breaking it down, the former took about twenty minutes, and the latter could take up to an hour.

After dinner, we bundled up into down coats and winter hats for the chilly desert evening. The park provided a large, open jeep and driver for the night safari. We, and eight others, were each given a blanket and a bright flashlight with a red bulb setting. This allowed us to see the animals without scaring them away.

Given my naïve hope of spotting the Big Five (lion, leopard, elephant, rhino, and Cape buffalo), our first safari experience was a bit disappointing. That night we saw numerous sets of golden eyes, and the guide pointed out several kangaroo-like, grazing rodents called springhares, a few black-backed jackals, and a fox or two. My excitement perked at one point when the guide called our attention to a "Southern African Wildcat." However, the pet-sized kitty looked laughably out of place to me, like a sassy tomcat from your Aunt Pat's house trying to act natural in the savanna.

The next morning we were up before dawn. We'd read that the animals are most active overnight so our best chances of seeing them were at sunrise and sunset. This meant we'd need to have a quick start each morning, a midday break, and then head out again in the late afternoons if we wanted to spot the wildlife.

Dave and Paige, who always woke up hungry, saved sausages from the night before to have as their breakfast. I was the opposite, never hungry first thing. Freakishly, Dave and Paige also didn't drink coffee, but I hadn't started the day without two cups since age 20. I was gastronomically outnumbered.

"Ame, would you mind having your coffee later in the day? It takes so long to boil the kettle," Dave asked expectantly.

"Ha! Good one," I laughed.

My face fell as I realized that he was serious.

It was early in our two-month trip together, and I was still trying to impress Dave's daughter with how flexible and considerate I could be.

"Sure," I agreed pleasantly…well, as pleasantly as a caffeine-addict can at 6 a.m.

Little did I know that this would become our new safari routine. *Bladdy Hell!*

I didn't know Paige all that well. Despite the fact that Dave and I had been together for a decade, Paige was a young adult by the time I met her, and she lived an exciting life of her own. A British travel blogger who had made the most of Commonwealth visas, by 28 Paige had lived in five countries, and had traveled to eight times as many. She was a hard woman to pin down. The few times Paige had come to visit us, between her ages of 19 and 28, she had been quiet, reserved, and no doubt still maturing as a person. We hadn't really connected as two women, but I hoped that one day we would find our way into friendship.

Dave was a devoted father. However, the African trip would be the longest he had continually spent with his daughter since the divorce from her mother, twenty years earlier. A military man, Dave spent most of Paige's childhood posted in the United States, but he visited her as often as he could in England or vice versa—perhaps four times a year. Of course, Dave was thrilled when Paige was free to join us in Africa. I had such a close relationship with my own dad, and it made me happy for them to be together. We were excited. I'd finally get to know Paige a bit better, and Dave would get to share this major life chapter with the most important women in his life.

Just imagine the adventure! What better way to connect than on an adult-family vacation, in a challenging place, with an exhausting itinerary, in two tents on top of a truck for two months! What high hopes we had for our little tribe.

I decided to drive our first safari morning so that Dave and Paige could take pictures. They were both avid photographers, and it was neat that they shared a father/daughter passion. I was grateful I could count on them to visually capture our trip. I hoped to do the same later in words, and I used my eyeballs and head holes in the meantime. Dave sat in front with me, and Paige took the back to have access to both windows.

We could see our breath in the truck the next morning. I cranked the heat up as we drove slowly along. We carefully scanned the red and silver-tinged grasslands as the golden sun rose over the horizon.

Not thirty minutes later, we noticed a collection of jeeps on the road up ahead.

"They must see something," I mused.

"Indeed. Let's go see," Dave added.

As we approached the vehicles, a juvenile male lion emerged from the left-hand roadside bushes and began to cross. He joined another male on the right. I drove up, angled our truck for the best photographs, and turned off the ignition. The inside of our vehicle went from shouts and squeals to shushing and clicking as we took in the majestic brothers. We had front-row seats, about 30 feet from the lions, for what felt like tickets to an 8 a.m. show.

The dangerous thing about lions, other than the fact that they will rip open your belly and play with your intestines while you're still alive, is that they look like giant house cats. Like big furry sirens, the cuddly boys in front of us were just begging to be scratched behind the ears. I wanted to use both hands to gently stroke up their delicate noses, over their eyebrows, and to grip into their manes. I had a strange urge to nibble the squishy pads of their great paws and massage down their spines, paying extra attention to that sweet spot at the base of the tails. I even felt tempted to tickle their bellies. And, dammit, I'm a dog person.

"Come play with us," they purred. "It's easy. Just open the car door."

I did manage to resist, but the brothers were spellbinding. We dutifully revered the royal pair until they'd had enough of our adoration. Satisfied or bored, they eventually stood, stretched, and lazily padded away.

"Well, that was easy," I joked afterward; my pupils still swirled like a hypnotized cartoon character.

Our beginner's luck lasted the entire day and part of the next as we made our way west toward Namibia. We managed to see two male and two female lions, a family of five cheetahs on the hunt, some giraffes, and a spotted hyena. The antelope-like "deery-things" were everywhere—springboks boinged along, while gemsbok and hartebeest grazed in the distance. That first small safari was the perfect primer for all that was to come.

The Fish River Canyon – Namibia

Driving into Namibia was desolate. Long, straight, wide, dirt roads cut through mile after mile of white sandy plateaus littered with green scrub. On the two-hour drive from the South African border to the first major city, Keetmanshoop, we passed four cars. If we weren't careful to go slow over the gentle swoops of road, Bucky caught air.

We'd come to Namibia to hike the Fish River Canyon. According to a few lists of 'World's Best Hikes,' the five-day trek through Africa's largest canyon would be an unforgettable experience. Dave and I had done lots of multi-day, hut-to-hut hiking through the years, but this was going to be our first backcountry trip, carrying our own tent and food deep into the bush. We'd purify our water each day from the river.

The Fish River Canyon was the largest canyon in Africa, located in the south of Namibia. After the Grand Canyon in the USA, it was the second-largest canyon in the world. At 161 km long (100 miles), 27 km wide (17 miles), and up to 550 m deep (1,800 feet), this enormous canyon features some of the oldest rocks in Namibia, cut by the Fish River over a billion years ago. We would be ants' ants in this primeval, massive gash in the earth.

Of all the excursions we'd planned for our two months in Africa, this undertaking worried me most. At that time, only 30 hikers per day were allowed into the canyon, and reservations were required. We'd booked the hike a year in advance, so I had low-grade anxiety for months as we geared up for the big event. Without guides, we would trek several days into one of the world's most remote regions. What could possibly go wrong? I wondered if we were approaching that line between intrepid and idiotic.

"Everything will be fine," Dave reassured me. "People have run ultra-marathons through the canyon," he added, as if this offered some comfort.

"Great! Someone can jog out with my remains next spring."

We traveled to the southern edge of Namibia using maps that we had downloaded in advance. The bossy lady who lived in our phone did a good job of navigating offline, but sometimes the direct routes we took were very sporty and driving times could be fuzzy. Occasionally, what Dave had carefully planned to be a five-hour drive might be incorrectly described on our phones as 30! This made for stressful driving, but I took comfort in the knowledge that we had Bucky, our self-contained vehicle. We'd get there eventually.

One week into our travels, we pulled into our campground for the Fish River Canyon. Meaning "burning waters" in the local dialect, the luxurious, albeit tired, Ai-Ais Resort featured a hotel, bush chalets, a full campground, a swimming pool, tennis courts, a spa, a restaurant and bar, and, best of all, thermal pools. Conveniently, it was the ending point of our five-day, four-night trek. So, we would be walking ourselves right back to well-earned, much anticipated hot springs and cold beers there at the oasis!

Once we'd set up camp, we pulled out our hiking backpacks and began organizing our belongings for the trek. Tents, sleeping bags, trekking poles, dehydrated meals, changes of socks and underwear, a blister kit, water purifiers, and other essentials scattered the ground as we situated ourselves.

At one point, a campground attendant came over to warn us.

"Be careful of the baboons. They will take your things," he cautioned.

I had long ago moved beyond the notion that 'monkeys are cute.' By then, I had both lived and traveled in places where primates were prevalent, so I already knew that monkeys were assholes. Baboons, which can weigh up to 30 kg (66 lbs) were downright dangerous. All fangs, nasty ass, and nuisance, I saw nothing to redeem them.

Later on that trip, another campground attendant would tell me that when school groups came to stay, the male baboons only harassed the girls' chalet, not the boys', because they could smell females. While neither the campground attendant nor I were Dr. Jane-freakin'-Goodall (*whom I adore and to whom I now humbly prostrate myself*), I trusted that he was speaking from firsthand experience. Plus, as both a feminist and a baboon bigot, I didn't need another reason to dislike these jerks.

I scanned the perimeter guardedly and brought my belongings a little closer to our tents.

The next morning started off early. Too early. Actually, we were ready with plenty of time to spare because none of us had noted the time change as we crossed into Namibia. We arrived for the 9 a.m. shuttle an hour before it was scheduled to leave.

Our campsite neighbors no doubt appreciated our clattering, unnecessary 5 a.m. wake-up. However, these same folks had kept us awake with their loud late braai the night before, so I didn't feel too bad. I did manage a little sympathy for them when, early the next morning, an enormous, alpha-looking baboon rifled through their camp kitchen, opened up their cooler, and drank an entire carton of orange juice while the humans slept. *Asshole.*

As we waited at the shuttle stop, I looked across the grass and saw a group of tall, thin, good-looking people, nine ectomorphs, packing up their tents. In their campsite, they looked like outdoor clothing models—beautiful, lean, young, white people with backpacks and hiking boots, laughing in the sunshine. One folded up a hammock, while two others threw a Frisbee. A gentle breeze blew through their sun-kissed locks.

Oh great, I thought. *I hope that's not them.*

Sure enough, the troop made their way over to the shuttle stop, fifteen minutes late, which in actual fact wasn't late because the driver was operating on African time. I was surprised to see that a few of the group had lined faces and one man even had a receding hairline. They still looked like models, just retired ones, who smoked. And, that's how I came to think of them over the course of the next few days—the Retired Models, the RMs.

Actually, they were perfectly nice folks, just overwhelming due to their large number, CONVERSATION VOLUME, and a shared ability to remain exceedingly attractive well into their thirties. After chatting with one of the women, we learned that they were a group of old friends from Cape Town, and over the years they had gone on several "missions" together. I liked that 'missions' made it sound as if they were trained assassins, not hikers.

In the shuttle, Paige, Dave, and I sat quietly, helplessly eavesdropping on their conversations. In front, one woman shared about a "dickhead" in her department, while a man in the back bragged about the "six-million-dollar deal" he was working on. They had distinctive South African accents, but spoke in English, not Afrikaans. I noticed that most of their speech was punctuated with 'Ja' not unlike my lazy 'yeah.' It reminded me a bit of 1980s American Valley Girl talk.

After a brief stop to register and to turn in our mandatory medical releases, we drove into a flat open horizon. The driver stopped in the dusty plain next to a gazebo where we unloaded our packs. We watched the shuttle drive away, and a gentle panic washed through my collarbones. There was only one way back now.

At the edge of the gazebo was an overlook. It was there that we had our first glimpse into the massive canyon. Before us, the cracked earth lay open, and a tiny, winding, dark green snake, the Fish River, dared us to follow. Naively, Dave, Paige, and I descended into the world's second-largest canyon.

The following five days and four nights were a blur of drudgery. Though we were seasoned hikers, the brutality of the terrain was astonishing. In hindsight, it's logical to reason that a canyon is made when earth erodes. However, at the time I was surprised by the sheer amount of boulders, loose rocks, and sand in the bottom. When we weren't teetering across shifting river stones, we were slogging through ankle-deep sand. There was no single 'well-worn path,' but rather squiggles left by individuals like us—masochists and their bewildered loved ones, all stumbling for 90 km (56 miles) in the same general direction.

And yet, the stars at night were among the brightest I had ever seen. The Milky Way was a crisp stripe in the sky. The canyon was incredibly dramatic, too, especially the first two days when it was at its narrowest. With steep, dusty cliffs towering overhead, the twisting, hunter-green Fish River guided us along. Our brief little lives were but a glimmer of sand in this immense, unfathomable expanse.

Soon everything hurt. We fell exhausted into our tents each night. At some point in the week, I realized that my innards had gelled together, like a bag of gummy worms left in the car on a boiling Texas summer day. In order to get my backpack to rest on my hips, I'd first press into and lift my belly, hoisting my congealed organs higher into my chest cavity before buckling the waist strap. It seemed to help.

To make matters worse, baboons plagued us. Okay, not really, but we did have a couple of unsettling encounters with lone males. One geriatric fellow lurked at the edges of our campsite the second night. Never making eye contact, he crept closer and closer, freezing like a statue when we glanced his way. To ward him off, I puffed out my chest, grunted around our territory, and threw purposely misaimed rocks at the old codger. He eventually decided to back away from our camp and especially me, the demented, androgynous female.

Another day, a virile male who was guarding his territory threatened us. Across the river, coming off a rocky hillside, I heard what sounded like the scream of an American mountain lion. In the distance, my eyes struggled to find the source until I saw the streak of his dusty coat. A baboon raced across the rocks and displayed, puffing his chest out and flashing his fangs. He made sure we knew that it was *his* canyon. Thankfully, we were very far away. For many reasons, including me never hearing the end of it, I would have regretted that time I pushed Dave into the path of a charging baboon in order to save myself. Fortunately, we were both spared.

Adding to our annoyance, we played leapfrog with the Retired Models throughout the canyon. Like Eagle Scouts, Paige, Dave, and I were well-prepared but laden with rain gear and extra layers that we never ended up needing. Fighting blisters, back injuries, and bad knees we trudged along, staying just ahead of vultures.

Meanwhile, the RMs made great time. Much fitter, taller, and with only biltong and bikinis in their packs, they were positively enjoying themselves. Occasionally, we'd hear a flurry of "Ja" and look over to catch a glimpse of beautiful bodies splashing in the river. I imagined that this was how they recharged their strength—with an invigorating dip, a doobie, and a quick revitalizing orgy. Refreshed, they inevitably caught up to and skipped passed us.

We did survive. Five days later, we made it back alive—older, wiser, and war-worn. Even years later, when reflecting on our time in the Fish River Canyon, I would still not be able to say that the hike was worth it. Agony outweighed awe. We all agreed that, physically, it was quite possibly the hardest thing each of us had ever done. (It ranked second for me, after a marathon in Portugal). However, I was proud of us for pushing our limits, and we would always have the satisfaction of having persevered. Best of all, like retired models, we'd accomplished our mission.

We spent a day at the Ai-Ais resort for a beer and burger recovery beside the pool. We did laundry, and Paige did yoga. I thought about doing yoga, but I journaled and ate ice cream instead. We cleaned out Bucky and just generally reset. It was the first of too few rest days on the trip, downtime all three of us would come to relish and crave.

Dave, a retired fighter pilot-turned-high school physics teacher, had planned the African portion of our year off. Like many of the schedules he created in life, his itinerary was astonishingly detailed, brilliant, but just the slightest bit brutal. It was designed to maximize as many highlights as possible from *The Travel Spreadsheet.*

The Travel Spreadsheet was a little something Dave put together as he approached retirement from the military, at age 45, after 27 years in the Royal Navy. He'd carefully read seven or eight of those humongous coffee table books, with titles like *Journeys of a Lifetime* or *Trekking Atlas of the World!* Then, using a 1-3-9 rating scale to rank through a series of variables such as "Natural Wonders, Man-made Wonders, Activities, Hikes (which merited its own category), and Distance from Hikes," the spreadsheet could be sorted by a number of factors. Dave had determined which countries in the world most warranted a visit, and what he most wanted to do, in almost any given country, for his remaining time on the planet. In the ten years we'd been living together, we'd crossed several goals off of his spreadsheet, which then, of course, recalibrated itself.

However, it would be a disservice to cast Dave as that flyboy from *Top Gun*, some uncompromising military Commander, or a nerdy scientist because he was a bit of all of those characters and none of them. A Renaissance man, Dave also restored a 100-year-old farmhouse himself, distilled vodka at home, and was a kickass DJ. Overall, when attempting to describe my life partner, I was reminded of my mom's best friend Vicky (a woman whose candor helped shape me into a kinder person, but that's another story). Aunt Vicky once said, "Amy, there are two types of people in the world: Tweakers and Fuck-Its. Keep in mind that one isn't better than the other; they're just different. *Tweakers* are the kind of people that like to fix things. They're the detail-oriented folks of the world, like Harry, who have the patience to stick with a project. (Aunt Vicky's husband was a luthier—he meticulously built and repaired stringed instruments such as guitars and violins.) *Fuck-Its*, on the other hand, well, you get the idea."

More than anything, my husband was a *Tweaker.* In Namibia, I began to see that his daughter was, too. I, however, was the other character type.

The Sossusvlei – Namibia

The next day, we headed north to the Namib-Naukluft National Park. Along the way we passed through pristine little towns with European names like Seeheim, Bethany, and Helmeringhausen. Easy and orderly, travel through Namibia was smooth but sterile. I couldn't see much evidence of a native Namibian culture that existed before colonization.

I wasn't the only person wondering about black culture. On hearing that I was American, one black shopkeeper asked me, "So, America doesn't have many black people?"

I stared dumbfounded for three beats.

"Oh yes! Yes, we do," I recovered, shocked by his misperception. "There are lots and lots of black people. They're everywhere! Well, except for, like, North Dakota."

He looked doubtful, given his personal experience. It saddened me to realize that he had rarely met African American tourists. I struggled to condense this terrible byproduct of white privilege into a quick, accurate, gas station explanation.

Not to mention what Dawn, my African American friend from university, had said. Like me, Dawn had the mouth of a sailor, but at the time she'd given up swearing for Lent, which had the added benefit of making her family and friends crack up. When I told Dawn about our vacation plans she half-joked, "Amy, black people don't take mother-luvin' 'camping holidays' to the mother-luvin' desert. Only white people do that shit—tockay. Shiitake. I don't want to *survive* my vacation; I want to *enjoy* it. I can be hot, tired, and uncomfortable here in turd-suckin Texas for free."

The man in the gas station had me gold-panning my thoughts. Given that he worked as a cashier, I figured he lived paycheck to paycheck. Moreover, obviously, he understood more deeply than I *ever* could what it was to be a person of color and to be tired of the extra struggle that went with it, irrespective of wealth.

I wish I'd said something like, "I think most black Americans would love to visit Africa, including your beautiful country Namibia, but many people in the United States, especially black people, do not have enough money or time off work for a big vacation like this."

Unfortunately, I was an awkward arbitrary ambassador, and those words didn't spring to my lips. Instead, my white ass nailed the moment with, "By the way, do you have an ATM machine?"

Situated in The Namib-Naukluft National Park, the Sossusvlei, meaning dead-end marsh, was a clay and salt pan surrounded by the largest sand dunes in the world. At heights up to 325 meters (1,066 feet), these distinctive red giants attracted thousands of (white and Asian) tourists each year. There we also planned to see the Deadvlei, an ancient white clay pan, which offered an almost alien landscape of scorched, dead, black trees on flat, white earth. An enormous red dune named Big Daddy towered in the background. Photographers came from all over the world to capture this iconic image.

"Oh great. More sand," Paige grumbled, as we approached the park in the late afternoon.

Our little jaunt through the canyon was still fresh in her mind.

We made our way into the park and got our bearings. That night we made a little drive to a nearby, nameless dune to watch the sunset. Dave and Paige snapped dozens of photos, and I sat quietly with my feet in the sand, watching the dunes change from burnt orange to sienna red to shadowed mauve.

The next morning, along with two hundred friends, we rose at 4:30 a.m. to climb Dune 45 for sunrise. We joined the beginning of what would become a long line of cars waiting for the park gates to open. Like many others, we were eager to be among the first so we could take photos without crowds. The atmosphere felt like the starting line of a 10K Run. However, the racers had to stay in a line and travel for forty minutes, in the dark, at the painfully slow, national park speed limit. By the time we arrived at the Dune 45 parking lot, Dave was positively frothing.

Dune 45 was impressive, but it wasn't any more remarkable than its siblings. We supposed that by having all the tourists climb it, all other dunes were preserved. And, it was near the road. Regardless, standing at 170 m (558 ft) the dune took most people forty minutes to one hour to climb up, and five minutes to come down.

The competition wasn't over. In the parking lot, we quickly found a spot since we were among the first cars to arrive. People spilled from their vehicles, and raced toward the still-dark dune. The sky was beginning to lighten in the east, and we still had almost an hour's hike to the top. There was no time to lose.

Dave and Paige grabbed the cameras from the truck, and we headed quickly to the trailhead. At the base of the dune, we ripped off our shoes and began our ascent up the crested spine of the dune. Unfortunately, because we'd arrived with the pack, we were still in a single file line, trying to keep pace with the person in front of us.

It soon shifted into a fitness contest. Having recently hiked through the canyon, I was something of an expert at slogging through sand. Climbing the sand dune was similar, but more delightfully difficult since it was uphill. For every step forward I slid a quarter-step back. We often got stuck behind slow people, but the elderly and out of shape pittered out quickly. Bent-over bodies gasped along the trailside, and I tried to avoid bumping them as I passed. If pushed too far either way, chubby little grandparents would have slid down the Dune 45 into oblivion.

Dave and Paige were in front, setting a fierce pace. That morning I'd gone without my coffee again, so I struggled to transition from the snuggly, warm truck into a cold, dead sprint up the side of a sand dune. Plus, Mother Nature chose that morning to kick in, and I developed possibly the worst menstrual cramps of my entire life. It felt like my pulsing uterus might inch out of my body and ooze down my pant leg. So, about 35 minutes into our hike, very near the top, I let Dave and Paige go on ahead. I gouged a seat into the sand near the path, moved my carcass out of the way. There, I cradled my twisting womb and ego. At the risk of sounding like an ol' country n' western song, I Lost My Uterus on Dune 45.

There, cushioned in the sand by myself and wiggling my toes in the silky grains, I witnessed the ancient dunes wake up to the light. As I watched the shifting colors, I took a moment in my mind to find my spot in the world. First, I saw me in the dunes, and zoomed out to picture my position in the map of Namibia. Next, I visualized Namibia within Africa, and then Africa, the Motherland of all humanity, centered on Earth. From there, I zoomed out again to look down on our entire planet, and then pictured it circling for sunrise. Finally, I flashed back to see me in the context of it all.

Amy was here, I smiled from deep within.

When that first slice of blinding light finally peeked over the dunes in the distance, I was filled with reverence. From my tiny sandy seat into the great universe beyond certainty, I sent a signal: *Thank you. Thank you. Thank you.*

The way down was much faster. I decided to try my luck on the gentle sand, hoping that my bad knees would cooperate for the descent. It was too steep to run directly downhill without toppling head over heels, so we aimed for a respectably wild angle. At full speed, Dave, Paige, and I bounded down one of the world's largest sand dunes, laughing the entire way. Beneath us, the sand squeaked with each step.

Back at Bucky, we finally made some coffee and had a second breakfast before heading to our next stop, the Deadvlei. In order to see this famous landscape, the white salt pan and dead black trees with the Big Daddy Dune in the background, tourists needed to drive about fifteen minutes through deep sand to the trailhead. This required a 4WD vehicle, or we could stop and pay a thorny fee to ride in a 4WD shuttle, which was driven by an expert. Since Bucky was a badass and we were misers, we decided to do it ourselves. We figured, what was the worst that could happen?

It turned out that there was a trick to driving in sand, and it wasn't to drive slowly and carefully. In order to stay on the surface of sand, a driver needed to keep their speed up and to slightly shift the steering wheel back and forth, a bit like a slithering, drunken snake. We learned this lesson the hard way.

We didn't get far. New to driving in sand, Dave started down the path cautiously, like a little old lady driving to church. It was good that he was behind the wheel because it freed up Paige and me to bark helpful commentary. Despite our great advice, we soon got stuck. Dave tried to get us free, but the wheels just spun as we sank deeper and deeper into the sand.

It was about then that it dawned on me that we were *stranded in the middle of an African desert!* Things started to get ugly. It's true that Paige had the best idea, to use the floor mats for traction; however, when we didn't try her plan immediately, she grew frustrated. And, like many adult children who have been in close quarters with their parents for a little too long, Paige was suddenly possessed by the spirit of her 16-year-old self. In turn, Dave had gone into a dictator's rescue mode, barking orders to an unconvinced, captive audience. Meanwhile, I froze up to breathe through a smidge of overzealous, ear-roaring panic. On our bellies under the truck, we used our hands to furiously shovel sand away from the tires, as we each tried, in our own ways, to feel more in control. To say the least, tensions were running high in our sweet little family, which, beyond the present crisis, had been living together in a "turd-suckin'" truck for two weeks.

I was beginning to see my friend Dawn's point.

Adding to the emotional spin, park shuttle drivers kept stopping to offer "help." The bakkie Bucky was buried up to its axles. Several times we'd almost cleared the sand away from the wheels when a park driver would come along with a safari vehicle filled with twelve tourists. He'd quickly jump out to give thirty seconds of help while jackass holiday-makers took pictures of our plight.

"You need to rock it, like this," every driver suggested.

He'd then stand on the front bumper and bounce our vehicle back and forth from side to side in an effort to shift away the sand. Each time, the driver's aid ended up undoing all the hand shoveling we'd already done. He'd shrug his shoulders and hop back in his waiting shuttle. The tourists would snap a few more photos as they rode away, leaving us to start all over again.

Eventually, there was a break from all that assistance, and we were ready to try Paige's idea. We cleared the sand as best we could and placed the floor mats in front of the wheels. Paige got in the driver's seat because at 5'2" (157 cm) and a hundred-n-nothin' (45 kg + not much), she was the smallest. Dave and I, the husky parents, pushed from behind.

"One, Two, Three!" Paige counted out the window, and hit the gas.

The wheels grabbed onto the floor mats and the vehicle clambered free. Sand and mats spit out in every direction. One narrowly missed my shin. Paige kept up the speed, so she wouldn't get stuck again and made her way to firmer ground. We were finally out, thanks to her ingenuity.

Afterward, we were exhausted, and the afternoon winds had picked up, so stinging sand was blowing into our eyes and ears. We decided to turn around to have some lunch, nap, and try again a few hours later.

After we regrouped, we headed back to the Deadvlei entrance. I had reservations about making the sandy drive ourselves, and I was willing to pay for the shuttle. I'd spent too much time up to my armpits in sand that morning. As an added bonus to the ride, I figured, we'd get some good pictures of our driver and bickering families digging their own vehicles out of the sand. However, Dave and Paige both wanted to go for it. My companions needed to conquer the Sossusvlei; I only needed to savor it. I was outvoted. *Oh screw it*, I sighed to myself. *With the right attitude, I can cherish this vacation from underneath the wheels of a 4x4.*

"Okay. Let's do it." I agreed.

Dave got off to a good start, maintaining strong speed and a slight zig-zag. As Dave white-knuckled the steering wheel, Paige and I were uncharacteristically quiet. We knew he needed our silence to concentrate.

There was no distinct path through the sand, just a general direction. The few times we did follow in the exact tire grooves of a previous vehicle, Bucky, and then my heart, would slowly begin to sink. Dave would quickly adjust. Occasionally, a shuttle might pass us on the right or left, moving in the same or opposite direction. Sweeping between low trees and brush, we did our best to avoid the deepest looking lakes of sand and other trucks. The only traffic rule seemed to be "Don't Get Stuck!"

Five long minutes stretched to ten. It felt like days. Dave's hands and arms stayed clenched and his speed stayed fixed the entire time. He began to sweat. Paige and I stayed quiet, unless to softly encourage, "You're doing great, Dave," or "Good job, Dad." For years to come, I would hold this image of him in my mind. It captured almost everything I loved most about Dave.

He did it. Eventually we made it to the parking lot on firm ground, and all breathed a huge sigh of *half* relief. After we toured the area, we'd still have to get back. And thankfully, Dave made that happen too.

The Deadvlei was striking, unearthly, and absolutely worth the trouble it took to get there.

As tempting as it might be to outline a damning plot of my perceived offenses and then craft a tale with me starring as the Vacation Victim, you won't find that character in this story. To my growing surprise, Paige and I were a lot alike. And, while she might not have seen it at the time, at 40 in Africa, I wasn't so very far from my late twenties. I could remember what it was like to spend time with my parents as a young person, fighting to be seen and treated as an adult while the teenager inside me could still rear her pimply head. I understood the compassionate impulse to improve one's mother—to update her frumpy outfit and to monitor her diet Coke consumption because *the woman so clearly needs my help.* Or, I could understand how one might finally snap on an extended Christmas vacation, for example. How said person might find herself shouting "You never listen to me! Quit treating me like a child!" as she slammed her old bedroom door, only to hear her beloved parents quietly chuckling from the living room. I mean, you know, for example.

Mind you, I had the best parents a person could ask for—funny, loving, supportive people who are still married and each other's best friend. However, relating to those two in my twenties was like climbing a sand dune —two steps forward, one step back, and best done with plenty of coffee (or alcohol). I felt for Paige in Africa, and I understood her growing exasperation with us, her unforgivably cringey, middle-aged companions. However, not having helped to raise Paige, I struggled to adapt to my new role in the arrangement (a supporting one) and to embrace the joys that came with stepmotherhood. *Evil stepmotherhood*, on the other hand, now there was something I began to think I could work with.

The Skeleton Coast – Namibia

We left the *Sossusvlei* and headed north up the Skeleton Coast. Historically, Bushmen called that region "The Land God Made in Anger" due to the inhospitable terrain and climate. Portuguese sailors had referred to it as "The Gates of Hell," because while ships were able to access the shore, the surf was too strong, in a time before motors, to launch back into the sea. The only way out was through the desert, the one God had made in anger.

In recent history, the Skeleton Coast was named for the seal and whale bones from the whaling industry that littered its shores. However, we went to see the skeletal remains of shipwrecks, those caught by offshore rocks in the fog. The sea had reclaimed most of the wreckage by the time we visited in 2017, but we were still able to see the red rusted bones of the Dunedin Star, which ran aground in 1942.

We also went to see fur seals at the Cape Cross Seal Reserve. We smelled them before we saw them. The colony was enormous—tens of thousands of lumbering brown fur seals, all barking or napping in one massive, rancid pile. They scattered as we crept nervously along, "protected" by a walled boardwalk. The seals were surprisingly timid for creatures that could outweigh Dave by 100 lbs (45 kg). The sheer quantity of animals was visually numbing, like a seal version of a *Where's Waldo* scene. At the edges of our silly cartoon, black-footed jackals licked their chops and scanned for a distracted mother and her stinky fat pup.

We left the seal colony and headed inland toward Etosha National Park. By this point in the trip we'd done about 1, 900 miles (3,000 km) in Bucky, and except for a short pussyfoot to the boardwalk through panicking seals, I'd gone perhaps 36 hours without questioning if we might, you know, perish. To keep me from slipping into a false sense of security, there in the desert that God made in anger, Bucky blew out two tires, about an hour apart. Thankfully, we had two spares.

When the first one blew, Dave knew exactly what to do. So did I. We'd lived together for nine years by this stage, and I'd grown passive and subordinate in these situations. To the untrained eye, I might look rather useless or perhaps lazy. Actually, it wasn't that I didn't have initiative, but, even in times of low stress, Tweaker Dave was a very particular man. I'd begrudgingly learned to follow orders or stand aside at times like these. My flair was best used in other ways.

Paige, however, was her father's daughter. More interested in being involved and not actually married to the jackass, she elbowed right in there to problem-solve with her dad. Anyone driving by would have seen the two of them cooperating beautifully and me relegated to the sidelines.

Relieved of my position, I sat roadside in the dirt, playing with sticks, and staring into the desolate horizon. At one point an ominous black and white crow came along to stare at me. If the tire change went badly, the bird planned to peck out my eyes and carry away my soul.

"*Take those two instead,*" I whispered to the crow.

Sometime later, in the distance, bakkies approached. A South African family stopped to check on us. They were in three vehicles, wisely following each other in caravan fashion. They'd arrived at a good time because we'd hit a small snag. The nut holding the tire to the back door of Bucky would not come undone so the spare was stuck on the truck. Dave would have managed it eventually, but when added muscle arrived, he didn't turn it down.

Out piled two parents about Dave's age, mid-fifties, and their five grown children and partners. Several young men jumped in to help Dave while the rest of us, mostly women, stood aside and chatted. Come to find out, they'd done several bush country adventures in the region. I hypocritically bristled at how we'd fallen into traditional gender roles with the men fixing the car and the women making sandwiches. Hell, *even I* knew the steps to change a tire. However, for the sake of efficiency, I refrained from rolling up my sleeves and swaggering into the sausage party. Mostly, I just appreciated these kind folks, and we were back up and running in no time.

"I'm just curious," I asked the dad as we parted ways. "About how fast have you guys been driving?"

"Oh, no more than 80 kph (50 mph). And be sure to switch on the four-wheel drive. Tourists lose control and crash on these dirt roads all the time. Why? How fast have you guys been going?" he answered and asked.

"Oh good. About the same," I lied. We'd been going 100 to 110 kph (60 to 66 mph) for weeks, not bothering with 4WD.

We slowed down and turned on the 4WD, but an hour later the second tire blew. Again, the South Africans came along behind us, but Dave and Paige were just finishing up. This time, because we were now out of spare tires, we joined their caravan. The family escorted us to the nearest town, which was luckily on their way, and we were able to replace one of our tires. Between Ernie and Elmian and this incredibly helpful family, South Africans had forever secured a special place in my heart.

With all the tire delays, by the time we arrived at Etosha National Park they had just closed the gates for the evening. To protect all the animals that came out at night, the park didn't want tourists driving in the dark so we missed our campsite reservation. Luckily, there was still an attendant at the gate who suggested a campground down the road.

Darkness was beginning to creep in, but we eventually found the road signs and made the slow shadowy drive through the bush to an open campsite. As we began to set up, the campground attendant Trever came by. We discussed the amenities and paid.

"Oh, and be careful of lions," he added as an afterthought.

"I beg your pardon," Dave stammered.

"Lions. They come around here sometimes. But don't worry; just shine your light. If you see a lion, don't get out of your tent."

I had a toddler's bladder, so I was typically up in the night at least once, if not two or even three times. However, by the time the next morning rolled around, I had taken on a golden hue. For years to come, I wouldn't be able to exit a tent without first checking for glistening golden eyes. It was one thing to understand a concept in theory, but I'd been viscerally reminded that we, arrogant humans, are *not* the top of the food chain.

Etosha – Namibia

The Etosha National Park was regarded as the gateway to northern Namibia. "Etosha," meaning "great white area," referred to a salt pan, the largest in Africa. It covered an enormous portion of the park's northernmost territory and was even visible from space. This unique and diverse landscape was home to a huge variety of animals including four of the Big 5: elephants, rhinoceroses, lions, and leopards. The buffalo was said to be missing, but I would later swear we'd seen them, too. Regardless, cheetahs, hyenas, giraffes, two types of zebras, blue wildebeests, red hartebeests, and dozens of other animals astounded visitors within the sanctuary. For me, our six-day safari through Etosha was the highlight of our entire African adventure.

Having survived the night, the next morning we headed to the park, which was to open at 6 a.m. We were running a bit late and arrived half an hour behind schedule; however, the employees didn't arrive until 7 a.m. There, waiting outside the gates, Dave passed the time by pacing and sighing with outrage, getting Paige and me worked up in the process. He was excited, in full safari mode, only missing the khaki shorts, cargo jacket, and wide-brimmed hat. At one point we debated the pros and cons of just barreling through the gates. Let's just say, our family was still adjusting to African time.

Once we'd finally paid and entered the park, we used the pamphlet they'd given us to race to the nearest watering hole. We were held in check by aggravatingly low speed limits, but we respected them because we knew they protected the animals. The watering holes, especially in the dry winter season, offered the best opportunity to see both big and small animals. Both natural and man-made, each watering hole had its own character and drew thirsty animals out from hiding in the bush.

Once again we were charmed with the most incredible beginner's luck. As we approached our first watering hole we were the only vehicle in sight. This wasn't generally a good sign because crowds tended to gather around the action. However, sipping at the water's edge was a mother lion with *five juvenile cubs*!

And we had the show to ourselves.

Awkward adolescents, these silly cats made us laugh out loud. With softer fuzz and a lighter color than full-grown lions, the sand-colored felines practiced their skills. Play-fighting pairs romped and wrestled. Others made ridiculous attempts to stalk much wiser birds. One cub chased his own tail and then annoyed his long-suffering mother by swatting hers. We watched them as long as they let us, for what felt like an hour. However, in their presence, I was so present that the time could have been much shorter. Eventually, the mother turned and made her way back into the bush, and her pride of ungainly teenagers asserted their independence by following loosely behind.

And the day wasn't over yet.

We worked our way through the roads and scoured the dusty plains for wildlife. Along the way we spotted hundreds of deer-like animals. While distinctive, the springboks, bushbucks, impalas, dik-diks, elands, hartebeests, and wildebeests never captured our interest for long, especially that first morning in Etosha. I felt sure we were letting down antelope specialists the world over. I pictured scholarly, sporty women and gangly, bearded men in fishermen vests filled with teeth and turds. They shook their heads in disappointment as we sped past. *You fools!*

Later that morning we struck gold again. This time we'd arrived at a watering hole that was almost entirely dried up. A small family of four elephants had stopped for a drink. There were only two other cars nearby, and we pulled into our own quiet space and turned off the ignition. We were delighted to finally see African bush elephants because Paige and I had something in common: the elephant was our favorite animal.

The largest land animal on Earth, and the longest-living land mammal next to man, African elephants could live up to 70 years in the wild. Wise, powerful grandmothers, who had more life experience than me, led families of females on migrations over 60 miles (100 km). Also, they were extremely sensitive. I'd seen documentaries of distressed herds protecting baby elephants by chasing off lions or problem-solving for hours to pull a stuck calf from the mud. I knew, for example, that sisters competed for the prized position of Auntie, all eager to take care of the babies. I'd even seen programs that showed elephants walking quietly, respectfully through the bones of other elephants. Essentially, of all the animals, it seemed to me that elephants had souls.

Years before, when I lived in Thailand, I'd visited and volunteered with Asian elephants often. In my ignorance, I'd been on an elephant ride before the Elephant Nature Park educated me about "the crush," the horrific process of torturing the spirit out of these majestic animals. The complex problem of elephant conservation soon became an issue I cared about. How could it not? After hugging month-old elephant babies and falling asleep to the deep rumbling comfort of an elephant mother singing to her child at night, I'd grown to adore these sympathetic giants.

However, I'd never seen *African* elephants in the wild. I knew that they'd be bigger, with larger ears, more rounded heads, and the females could also have tusks. I also knew that African elephants were said to be more unpredictable and potentially more aggressive than Asian elephants, but I wasn't worried. Yet.

That day at the watering hole we watched the elephant family, a bachelor group of males actually, drink water and apply sunscreen by tossing dirt onto their backs. Several antelope grazed nearby. The morning was getting late, and all creatures were feeling ready for naps.

Suddenly the animals stirred, and I happened to glance over my shoulder. Approaching quietly from behind was a black rhinoceros! He was made of bulging stocky muscle, was grey-colored, and had two horns. He was almost too close for us to move the car, and the photo opportunities were so fantastic that we decided to stay. We also knew that rhinos had terrible eyesight, and we figured that sitting still would be better than startling him with the ignition and a sudden blur of movement.

He slowly made his way toward us, stopping to sniff the air and refocus his tiny blinking eyes. Thankfully, he decided that we weren't a threat and decided to forgo ramming Bucky onto its side and trampling our family. Instead, he walked around the front of our vehicle, perhaps 50 ft (15 m) away, and headed to the water. The poor guy was just thirsty.

One of the elephants didn't see it like that. A large male began to flap his ears, ground stomp, and trumpet. It was a clear warning to back off. He then put himself between the water and the rhino, both challenging and then chasing back the slightly smaller beast.

Paige made us chuckle as she narrated what was happening.

"Oh great. Steve's had too much to drink again. Steve, stop it! For Christ's sake, just let the guy get a pint."

Eventually, Steve and other the elephants had their fill and moved on. Finally, the poor thirsty rhino was able to belly up to the bar.

The scene was a perfect example of what I grew to love most about being on safari: the little vignettes. It wasn't just about ticking off a list of animals as they were spotted, although we did want to see absolutely everything. For me, the best part of the safari experience was watching these miniature stories unfold.

Like the animals, in Etosha our lives fell into a pattern around the sun. Each day we'd wake early about 6 a.m., pack up Bucky, and safari from sunrise to almost 11 a.m. It was winter in late June, and temperatures reached approximately 80°F (27°C) so we'd find a spot to relax for the midday hours. The weather seemed perfect to me, a Texan, but my British husband and the African animals were more sensitive to heat. In the afternoons, we ate lunch, read, wrote, edited photos, and just generally siesta-ed. When the day began to cool, we headed back out around 3:30 p.m. just as the wildlife began to stir.

The park was large, and over the course of six nights we slept in three different campsites, combing our way from west to east across the park. We grew familiar with the map, and we ended up with favorite routes and watering holes. Rather than driving aimlessly, we often drove to one of the watering holes and waited. We'd read our books to pass the time as we waited for a character to enter the scene.

I seemed to have a knack for knowing where the animals would be. In everyday life, when I had a hunch about something, I liked to say "I feel it in my *bone*" not the plural *bones* because I was rather fixated on my imaginary "divining penis." Not unlike a real penis, it often steered me wrong, but it brought me so much pleasure. In Etosha, I had a magic touch, real strokes of telepathy, when it came to finding animals.

I did worry that announcing that I felt something in "my bone" might make Paige uncomfortable. I didn't want to make her think of parent sex, so I forced the "s" sound onto the end of what was otherwise a staple sentence in my life.

"Let's try that watering hole to the north!" I might say. "I feel it in my bones."

For the sake of Dave's fraying daughter, who was plumb worn out from supervising our "crisp" consumption, the volume and rate of Dave's breathing, and my woefully insufficient walking pace, I suppressed my nerdy pun and a strong urge to thrust my ancient crotch in cardinal directions.

Something was working for me. Even Paige acknowledged that I seemed to have a gift for knowing where the animals would be.

Paige had a gift, too. The woman was fearless.

One day we came across a group of vehicles gathered in a circular drive, always a good sign. We pulled into the mix, and soon a male lion came sauntering by. He walked down the road between the cars, daring anyone to question his ownership of the lane.

We'd been told that humans were safe inside their vehicles because the lions couldn't distinguish the people inside from the size of the overall shape. We'd often witnessed open safari Jeeps, filled with tourists, pull right up to lions and other wildlife. It seemed that as long as people stayed quiet, they were relatively secure.

Our windows were down, as the lion passed. Dave and Paige furiously clicked away with their cameras. I just sat taking it all in with my real eyeballs.

Suddenly, the lion paused at our vehicle and refocused, like a housecat who suddenly realizes there is no top on the fish bowl. I watched understanding wash over the feline's features as he approached the car.

"Uuuuh, Dave, Paige!" my voice raised. "Guys, please roll up your windows!"

They didn't seem worried behind the lenses of their cameras. Paige was the closest. I bet that she and the lion could smell each other. The lion's head cocked to the side, and his eyes widened with recognition.

Dave finally sensed the danger and quickly put up his window.

"WINDOW! PAIGE, PLEASE! I screeched.

"PAIGE!" Dave's bellow joined mine.

So much for the quiet keeping us safe.

At the last second, after a final photograph, Paige calmly raised the window. Human snacks obscured, the lion lost interest and moved away. She turned to shrug at us both.

"What? I had to get the photo for my blog, Dad."

Our next stop was the nearest bathroom so I could change my pants.

We grew incredibly spoiled as we went. The first time we saw a herd of giraffes, for example, we stopped for an hour, soaking in their gentle gangly majesty. It was the same for all the zebras, those stocky punks with mohawks; they were fascinating, at first. However, as the days unfolded we came to realize how numerous these creatures were. Eventually, we sped past the more common animals for fear of missing out on those we had yet to see.

To help us identify all the wildlife, we'd purchased a book of animals from one of the camp stores. Inside were illustrations of common animals in Etosha. One page showed and labeled dozens of different birds, another cats, and another of all the antelope-like herd animals. Of course we wanted to see absolutely everything possible, but we tried to balance this urge with what presented itself to us. Slowing down to appreciate all the different birds, for example, was quietly rewarding, too.

Sometimes, though, we'd go ages without seeing anything special. Being on safari was funny in that way. A few seconds of awe made up for hours of mediocrity.

One day we came across a tornado of tiny black and yellow birds. There must have been tens of thousands of them, whooshing through the air in tight, well-coordinated swoops. In unison, they changed direction in tight arcs, their small wings flashing black, yellow, black, yellow. It was spellbinding, but I couldn't help but notice those on the fringe—those awkward birds who couldn't cut it, messing up the formation with their bad timing and sloppy form. If it had been a competition, those beak-holes would be the ones to cost the team a medal.

After weeks on the road together, camping with Dave and Paige reminded me of the birds. The two of them buzzed around furiously, each with their own clear purpose—to wash the dishes, to reorganize the backseat, or to light the camp stove, assemble ingredients, and serve dinner. They worked together in a mesmerizing, relentless harmony, sometimes on the same task and other times on two or three different, simultaneous tasks. It was a hypnotizing rhythm, one that I couldn't quite follow.

I'd get out the butter only to discover one of them already put cooking oil in the pan.

"Here's a spoon for the mustard," I'd try.

"Oh, actually, I already have one here."

One day, my eyes began to glaze over as the two of them discussed the merits of various camera settings, so I took initiative and began folding down the tents for the night.

Crunch!

"...Uhm, did you remember to take out the camping chairs first?"

Shit.

"Brilliant. Well done, Amy!"

Ouch.

Sadly, our team didn't place that year in the Family Camping Championships.

Too soon, our six days in Etosha National Park came to an end. We'd managed to catch glimpses of every animal on our list, although that elusive leopard had blended into the trees too perfectly. We'd also witnessed the tale of a mother rhinoceros trying to cross the road with her baby, heartbreaking moments from the final hours of a giraffe's life (it had broken its ankle, the bone was exposed, and night was coming), and the love story of two lions, honeymooning by the pond.

We exited the gates, leaving Etosha National Park behind us in a cloud of dust from those Namibian dirt roads. I grabbed Dave's hand and just held onto it for a while. Paige wore her headphones in the backseat. We bounced down the dirt road, each quietly lost in our own thoughts.

My heart was full, but there was also that familiar beat of sadness, the slowing rhythm of something special coming to an end. I knew that the three of us were in the middle of one the greatest experiences of my entire life, and this part was over.

After a while, I turned to Dave.

"You know, Sir. That leopard didn't really count," I tossed.

"You think so? Perhaps we'll come back one day?" He batted back, knowing exactly what I wanted to hear.

When he said *perhaps* it always sounded like "paps." I'd taken it onboard.

"Paps. Paps, you're onto something," I sighed.

I smiled, squeezed his hand, and turned to look out the windshield.

The Okavango Delta – Botswana

The Okavango Delta was an enormous river delta in Northern Botswana. Each year a gazillion cubic tons of rainwater from the Angolan highlands flooded into the parched Kalahari Desert, submerging the trees and grassland in the process. During the dry season, thousands of animals were attracted to the delta, one of the only sources of water in the area. Consequently, the Okavango Delta became 'an Eden' for one the largest concentrations of wildlife and for tourists in the southern African region. In winter, however, numbers of the latter were blissfully low. We almost had the place to ourselves.

"If you need to do business, you can go over there, in that little building," said Chief, our guide who pointed toward several corrugated tin shacks.

I wondered if I might need to buy some cheesy puffs for our journey, but then realized that when Chief said "business" he meant the bathroom. It was there that I discovered my 'Second Worst-ever Toilet,' an impressive accolade since I had lived in developing countries for the better part of a decade.

When I returned from the bathroom, thwarted, I saw Dave and Paige standing at the water's edge near some modern, fiberglass boats. In my mind, I'd thought we'd be in traditional, wooden, dug-out mokoros, but quickly realized that it was a foolish, possibly racist and certainly classist, underestimation on my part. *Jeeze, Amy. You are the ignorant one here. Do better.* The contemporary mokoros were longer lasting than the older boats, but had a very similar profile, riding very low in the water.

There on the shore, Chief introduced us to his colleague Lily, who would pilot the second boat. After a quick chat, we decided that Dave and Paige would ride together with Chief, and I volunteered to go with Lily and our bags. I thought Dave and Paige might enjoy some father/daughter time. Chief's boat launched into the water first, and Lily and I followed.

Lily was the first woman from Botswana that I'd ever met, and I liked her natural vibe immediately. A black woman, she had a quick smile and the down-to-earth confidence of a woman who had a family to feed. It was obvious she had grown up in financial poverty because she was missing most of her teeth. I respected that she had freed her 'girls,' going braless under her t-shirt. However, this made it clear that she had carried and nursed the five children she proudly mothered, the oldest of whom was 23, I'd soon learn.

We chatted a bit as Lily poled our mokoro along, balancing with ease in the stern of our boat. She handled the canoe with finesse because she had spent her life on the water, first learning to steer at age seven. Lily spoke to me in choppy, intermediate-level English because it was probably her third or fourth language. She explained that she was happy it was her turn on the guide roster because this trip would bring in some extra money. I respected that she was sporty, like me. The two of us seemed to be about the same age.

In fairness to Lily, she could have viewed me through a similar lens. She might have seen before her a tall, androgynous, white woman with a serious, almost unkind face that utterly transformed with a crinkled, leathery smile. With my strong, pear-shaped body, yellow eyebrows, and matching, unnaturally straightened teeth, I would have appeared to have one grown child: Paige. Lily might have wondered if I had other children, and she might have felt surprise, or perhaps pity, to learn that I'd just never gotten around to wanting or having my own.

It would have been clear that I was interested in Lily because I peppered her with questions about her life in Botswana. I hope she sensed that I liked her, but my severe face and awkward, overcompensating social skills, which both stemmed from shyness, often worked against me. I could be a difficult one to read. A bit like an uneasy pit bull at the pet adoption fair; I might make a fantastic companion, but there was that unfortunate possibility that I might, oh I don't know, tear a person's face meat off their head bone. Plus, there was all that play biting. My humor often nipped a little too hard. When it came right down to it, I needed to be loved, but could I really be trusted?

My own mother joked that I was an acquired taste, so Lord knows what Lily made of me. But I'd bet my life savings that she spent a lot less time worrying about what people thought of her.

Speaking of animal violence, as Lily pushed us along that morning, I found myself wondering about hippopotamuses. I'd read that they were a serious risk in the Okavango Delta. On average, the dainty females weighed in at 3,000 lbs (1,400 kg), while the males could be anything from 3,500 to just over 9,000 lbs (1,600 to 4,500 kg)! They were extremely unpredictable, aggressive, and territorial, and, if things weren't spicy enough, they often made their homes in the same waters that humans used. In fact, Chief would later tell us, the hippopotamus was the most dangerous animal to man in Africa.

Hippos were known to charge and attack boats, especially small boats, like mokoros, which could be easily capsized. Passengers could be injured, killed, or drowned by the creatures. While planning for our trip I'd read to be especially careful in the narrow reed channels of the Okavango Delta, where there was no easy escape route for man or beast.

Lily didn't seem too concerned.

With Lily at the stern, floating through the Okavango Delta was one of the most serene experiences I'd ever had. Walls of tall green papyrus reeds surrounded us, hiding us within a magical water garden. As the mokoro parted the stalks, they gently thwacked against the boat and brushed, clacking gently, down the sides. The water trickled soothingly each time Lily lifted her long pole to push the boat forward.

Sometimes, I dangled my hand in the crisp, crystal clear water and scanned the mysterious flooded world below its surface. I was careful not to grab the reeds because Chief warned they could slice our hands. Through a maze of narrow channels, we silently made our way. Lily and I followed closely behind Paige, Dave, and Chief to a tiny island where we would camp for the night.

We disembarked and set up our tents while Chief dug a latrine. Once we were all set up, it was suggested we rest for a couple of hours because we would go on a walking safari in the afternoon. I wasn't tired, so I scouted out our immediate area, and soon discovered where they'd parked the boats. Chief was there and suggested that I give piloting a try. He went to tell the others.

There first and alone, I climbed into the nearest boat to test my balance, rising with a wobble to stand in one of the mokoros. I poled back and forth a foot or two, but I wasn't very steady. I didn't have a good feeling in my *bone*. Plus, when I imagined the discomfort of drying out, I decided not to risk falling in.

When Dave and Paige came, however, they were more game. They carefully climbed into the sterns of two different boats. Each trembled and quivered, jerking slowly into the center of the waterway, where they immediately got stuck in the reeds. In those long canoes they managed to block each other in, knocking their boats and poles together as they tried to turn and to free themselves. They wobbled and shrieked and laughed together. Watching Dave and Paige in that moment, I could see how much he loved her. I grabbed the camera to try and capture it all—the chaos and their connection.

I was equal parts relieved and disappointed when they both made it back to shore, exhausted and smiling, but dry.

Later, Chief started our bushwalk with a safety talk. There at the edge of a marshy field, he stressed the importance of quiet, and suggested we snap our fingers instead of calling out if we saw wildlife. Chief said our goal was to visit animals without disturbing them, so we would never get too close or move too quickly.

An experienced river bushman, Chief looked the part of a guide in his camouflage canvas jacket and cargo pants. He was a tall, strong, black man—perhaps 35 years old. I loved that he sported a soft drawstring American football backpack—the Kansas City *Chiefs*, of course. He was a slow-talking, thoughtful man, carefully considering his words before saying something worth hearing. I found Chief refreshing, comforting even, because he was clearly in touch with nature and the pace of life in the bush. He was full of facts. He knew the plants, their uses, and the animal scat. He was good at his job.

I had confidence in Chief, but I felt uneasy for the entire slow walk. We'd just been to Etosha and witnessed the size, speed, and power of African wildlife. It was one thing to observe them from the safety of our car, but the thought of approaching a wild elephant or hippo or, worst of all, a pack of lions on foot had me walking scared. My asshole stayed sucked up into my throat, like an Adam's apple, as we inched our way through the grassy open marshlands. My companions scanned the horizon so I watched our backs.

At one point, Chief pointed to a loose pile on the ground and said softly, "You see this? Hippo dung."

Chief explained that male hippos can curl their penises backwards. They then pee, poo, and rapidly flap their tails at the same time to create a 'poo shower.' It was how they marked their territory.

God, I wish I could do that, I thought.

I had a few flash fantasies of myself at children's birthday parties, at rival political rallies, and at unnecessary work meetings that should have been emails instead.

Chief knew that we were on a hippo hunt, so we were all encouraged to find signs of one. Dave and I had seen them before. However, after Etosha, the hippo was the last African animal on Paige's wishlist. We seemed to be on the right track.

SNAP! SNAP! SNAP! Chief urgently gestured that something was in the trees ahead. We all froze and looked. There, behind the branches in the distance, was a single male elephant, sweating at the temples.

"We must be very careful," Chief whispered. "Lone males are often in musk, and they can be dangerous."

He explained that musk was a part of the male elephant's reproductive cycle. During this time, bull elephants, especially the young ones, became highly aggressive because their testosterone levels were almost 60 times higher than normal! Their swollen glands could put pressure on their eyes and tusks. It was common to see lone males in musk digging their tusks into the ground, trying to relieve their migraines and toothaches. *Poor horny bastards.* Chief found a path to get us a little closer, but not too close. We watched for several minutes from what Chief deemed a safe distance.

The elephant was snacking on fruit under a palm-like tree. Tired of searching for fruit on the ground, he took matters into his own ivory tusks. As we watched, he placed a tall thin tree vertically between his two thick tusks. Then, he stretched his long trunk up the tree's trunk as high as he could reach. He rose up onto his hind legs and began to furiously shake the tree. Thunk, thunk! The fruit fell from high above, and he hopped down to feast on his bounty. The bull continued in this way, shaking the fruit from two or three more trees. Delighted, we all snickered a little too loudly at his ingenuity and impatience.

The elephant turned suddenly and looked up as if to say, "What are you lookin' at?"

Chief moved us safely away.

The elephant's antics had been one of my favorite-ever sights; however, we returned to our campsite a bit disappointed. Still no hippo. That night Chief told us not to leave our tents for any reason.

"What if I need to do business?" I asked.

"Do your business before bed," he replied. "Just don't get out."

All night long, splashing and the big-bellied, grunting of hippos' mocking laughter surrounded us.

The next morning, after a desperate trip to the latrine, we packed up our camp and climbed back into the mokoros. I was with Lily again, and our tranquil ride out was as magical as it had been coming in. She poled peacefully along for over an hour, and we approached the final bend before the main campground. I felt thankful for our experience, but a little disappointed for Paige.

Suddenly, we heard them! Deep grumbles of warning and splashes came from just ahead. Chief and Lily continued to pole our mokoros toward the noise, clearly not worried. My anxiety began to build as I imagined a hippo face off. The reeds opened into a wide waterway where two other boats of tourists were parked. Across the water, three chunky hippos waded, about 75 ft (25 m) away.

Grumbling insults, the hippos weren't happy to see us, but neither were they overly threatened. We seemed to be at a safe distance, next to the other boats, but the photos wouldn't be great. Chief decided to inch in a little closer, so Dave and Paige could get a better picture. I felt uneasy as I watched my husband and his only child peel away from the other boats and pole deeper into a hippo's territory.

"Lily, is it dangerous?" I squeaked.

"Yes. Dangerous!" she smiled delightedly.

I think she missed my point.

I'd seen the power of hippos before, from the safety of a large boat on the Ethiopian Lake Tana. I'd watched them launch their massive bulk up and slam back down with a hard, menacing splash. At the time, the waves had rocked our big boat, so I had little desire to watch it, to *feel* it again from a little, low mokoro. Worse, I had no desire to witness a hippo charge, capsize, and drown my loved ones. I asked Lily to take me on ahead to the final shore, where I worried, waded, and rehearsed what I'd tell Paige's mother if things went badly.

Ten minutes later, I felt relief when Chief, Paige, and Dave rounded the bend. Paige got her photos, alright. And, father and daughter were thrilled that Africa's most dangerous beast had given them a false charge.

Zimbabwe

Sure, I was an outdoorswoman, but I also enjoyed my comforts. I liked soft beds and hot showers, mascara and earrings, cappuccinos, foot massages, and drunk-shopping in little boutiques. So, as we pulled into Victoria Falls, Zimbabwe, a part of my soul sang *Hallelujah!*

Home to one of the Seven Natural Wonders of the World and its name-sake, the town of Victoria Falls was a tourist mecca. Restaurants, bars, shops, and spas offered giraffe steaks, craft beers, steam train rides, and facials. Shop-keepers and street peddlers hawked African masks, cute housewares, genie pants, and funky jewelry. With an airport of its own, Victoria Falls was the perfect way to "experience Africa" without getting your hands dirty. Some would call it a tourist trap, but for me, it was an oasis. We even splashed out for hotel rooms! We spent about thirty-six hours in Victoria Falls, but, after four weeks in a tent, I easily could have stayed longer.

Of course, the falls themselves were astounding, powerful, humbling—every fantastic descriptor a person would imagine them to be. We only visited from the Zimbabwean side, rather than paying over $100 in visa fees to cross into Zambia, but we didn't feel we'd missed out. It took us two to three hours to walk through sixteen viewpoints. I wished we'd brought raincoats and something to protect the cameras from the mist because, as the morning warmed up, we got soaked.

Disgracefully, by that stage in our travels, I was almost equally impressed by our dinner cocktails and being served breakfast on a restaurant patio. One afternoon the itinerary even allotted time for souvenir shopping! (Actually, I was just an indecisive browser who just talked herself out of purchases and regretted it later, but I loved to touch everything and encouraged my friends to spend money.) That day Paige and I window-shopped, while Dave haunted and exhaled from behind, a bit like having dog poop on my shoe. No, in fairness, my beloved was being a pretty good sport, and the three of us stopped in several little shops.

In one boutique, Paige tried on a cute African-printed dress. At 28, she looked 20, young enough to actually be my daughter had I started young. Beyond the natural beauty that comes with youth, Paige was a striking woman. She reminded me of a blue-eyed Hollywood starlet, the sort who made men crash bicycles into lamp posts. As if she needed to be any lovelier, Paige got uncomfortable when people mentioned her looks, preferring to be recognized as savvy or tough. I had been pretty in a farm-girl sort of way, but nothing like Paige. All heads turned when she entered a room.

Watching Dave's daughter model that dress made me remember my vacation in Japan the year before, when Asians and their superior collagen had surrounded me. One day I caught my reflection in the bathroom and all at once realized that my youth had finally slipped, and it was sort of *melting* off my face and neck. I'd always suspected I might be a little vain, but the aging woman in that Japanese mirror talked me through any lingering doubts. At the time I'd thought, *Well, hell. I guess I'd better get started on my personality.*

In Zimbabwe, as I looked at Dave's beautiful daughter rock that dress, a generous, maturing voice inside me thought, *Go get it, Paige! Enjoy every minute.*

It also whispered, *Buckle up, Amy. Your turn's not over. This shit's just getting real.*

Dave had to tackle and tie me to the passenger seat when the time came to leave the city. But, not far beyond its borders the spell broke, and I came back to my senses as we entered the park.

Hwange National Park – Zimbabwe

It was late afternoon and the third time we'd been to the salt pan. Other than yet another bushbuck in the distance, there was no wildlife in sight. Behind Dave in the backseat, I lowered my binoculars and huffed. It had been a discouraging couple of days.

"Shall we wait a bit and read our books?" Dave suggested.

We'd learned that quietly sitting often paid off.

"No. It's getting late, and I'd like to try that other place before the sun sets," Paige sighed and started the engine.

As she slowly rounded the curve, I noticed some movement over my shoulder.

"Y'all, wait! Look! An elephant," I perked.

We'd seen plenty of elephants in the last month, but after a day of almost nothing, at least this was something.

To the left of the car, about 75 feet (23 m.) away, a lone bull stood grazing. He was an adult, but I could tell he was young because he wasn't fully grown. I noticed he only had one tusk, which was unusual. He might have been sweating a bit at the temples. He was alone.

By this stage, I fancied myself an elephant guru, and I looked over at ol' One Tusk to read his body language. I knew that an elephant's ears were very expressive and could indicate mood, but I couldn't get a good sense of his disposition. He chewed slowly and seemed a little annoyed, like, "Can I please just eat my dinner in peace?" But, in my expert opinion, he didn't seem overly threatened or angry.

We watched for a minute, but Paige left the car running, not intending to stay long. She gently inched the truck forward. I rolled the window down and shifted myself halfway out the window to get a better view. My body waved around, outside the parameters of the vehicle. About that time, our wheels crushed a branch.

SNAP!

One Tusk startled and turned his hulking body to face the truck. In a flash, he started *charging toward us!* Turned out the window, I had a perfectly terrifying view.

"Go, go, Go, Go, GO, GO!" I shrieked to Paige. *"DRIVE!"*

Dave's voice joined mine.

Paige punched the gas! She hauled ass down that tiny forest road, bumping over that rocky, rooty, and worn-out lane. The Bucky, and we inside it, rattled in panic as we sped away.

A few seconds later, Paige began to slow, thinking the worst was behind us. I was still halfway out the window and looking back over my shoulder. There came One Tusk, still charging down around the bend.

"No, keep going!" I screamed.

He probably chased more than half the length of a football field, but Paige didn't slow down again for almost twice that distance. I didn't blame her.

When we finally pulled over, my heart was pounding so hard I could feel it in my anus. Adrenaline coursed through my limbs. Hell, adrenaline would course through my veins, years later, just writing about the memory.

In all my life, it was one of the most frightening, electrifying things I'd ever experienced.

Thereafter, when I looked back on the event, the "what-ifs" of that situation astounded me most. What if Paige hadn't left the engine running? What if the truck hadn't been faced forward, and she'd been forced reverse down that path? What if the elephant had actually hit the truck? Bucky was so top heavy with those tents, I'm sure we would have flipped onto our side. My God, we were so lucky—to have seen it and to have survived it!

From then on, I found it odd when lions were referred to as "The King of the Jungle." I no longer felt they deserved that title. Of all the animals in Africa, you don't want to *eff* with an elly.

Immigration – Zimbabwe

Immigration on the border between Zimbabwe and South Africa was incredibly efficient. As we pulled into the parking lot, attendants in reflective yellow vests guided us to several spots labeled "tourist parking" just outside the front doors of the building. Inside, the lines were short and well-organized, in part because of the employees standing at the door. One man asked to see our paperwork and directed us to the correct line, in much the same way an airline employee guided travelers through the check-in process at computer stations at an American airport.

Once inside a customs official told us that Dave, the driver, should also complete these forms and join that queue, but that Paige and I needed to wait outside in the truck. So we did. Inside, Dave was required to pay $30, but he didn't have the cash on him. So he returned to our car with the uniformed official. Paige happened to have our money, so she passed it over. We were given a receipt.

We were suckers.

Next, one of the "employees" escorted us to a line of cars, moving the cones aside when it was our turn in line. A bored looking man in jeans ambled over from a nearby building and took a quick glance inside Bucky, at weeks' worth of trip trash and at my hands, which still held our foreign passports. He motioned us to pass through the checkpoint, without search or comment.

On the other side of the checkpoint, our attendant indicated that we should pull aside and roll down the window. So we did.

"You need to organize something for us, my partner and me," he barked.

"I'm sorry?" Dave questioned, taken aback by the man's request and rude tone.

"We arranged for you to get through customs without a problem. You need to pay us. Hurry up. A bus is coming," the guy snapped.

Dave turned to look at me questioningly, wondering what I thought.

For context, Dave and I had worked as teachers in developing countries for most of a decade—Thailand, Bangladesh, and Ethiopia. We knew that in many societies, money greased the bureaucratic wheels, and that bribery was not only encouraged, it was required. For example, we once had a Bangladeshi friend who had to bribe the Bangladeshi man at the tax office to *let him pay* his property tax. The whole thing chafed against our personal code, but it had been our reality.

Through the years, Dave and I had learned how important it was to take care of the little guys, especially the nasty ones, because they were the people who could make you or break you. It wasn't that we didn't usually recognize when we were being exploited, although sometimes we did get scammed. Instead, Dave and I had lived much of our adult lives as white minorities with *relative* wealth, in foreign countries. It could be hard to judge when to stand your ground or suck it up.

"Dad, don't listen to him! He's lying!" Paige shouted from the back, her desperation curling into belligerence.

"Paige. Hold. On!" Dave barked back, needing time to think.

The two of them escalated, shouting, as did the man outside the window. Another man had come over to join, adding to the volume and chaos.

Meanwhile, I sat frozen. I wasn't sure which way to play it.

In the end, Dave handed the man $10, but the guy still wasn't satisfied. He demanded more money.

"*Ame! What do you think?*" Dave shouted at me, utterly stressed and needing me to help make the call.

"Just drive," I resolved.

Dave hit the gas, and sped away from the cursing man.

I prayed we wouldn't be pulled over because we were still inside the immigration compound. Prison in Zimbabwe had to suck.

At the exit gate, a final guard sat wearing that same "official" uniform, a yellow reflective vest and jeans. Part of me hoped Dave would accelerate, smashing through the barrier, but, of course, he stopped.

"So. How much did that crook get from you?" the guard asked, shaking his head.

"$10," Dave growled, all our doubts confirmed. "Why? You work here! Why did everyone just let it happen? Where are the police?"

The guard just shrugged his shoulders and opened the gate to let us pass.

With sheer relief, we left Zimbabwe.

It was an hour before any of us spoke. I think we all felt bruised and abused and stupid. Heavy metal blasted through Paige's headphones in the back. She seemed furious with us, yet again, for not listening to her.

Later, Dave and I realized the full extent of the con. Paige had been right about that demanding man at the car; however, our entire family had been taken for $40, not $10. That first man, the helpful one inside the immigration office who had ushered us through the process, had also been a thief.

What ached the most was that the woman behind the visa desk and those men at the vehicle checkpoints, *the actual immigration officials,* hadn't warned us. They'd just watched us get scammed.

Years later, when I combed through that memory again, the character I remembered most was a seemingly minor player—the second man outside our truck window, the one who came over to talk to the crook as we all argued. That man had been trying to appeal to the conman. A courageous person from a country so broken that police didn't police at immigration borders, he'd stepped up and in and tried to do the right thing. *I can see you now, Sir. Thank you.*

The lesson from that experience was never that Zimbabwe is "a shithole," or to generalize that Africa is a place to be pitied or feared. Sooner or later, a world traveler will bump into corruption because it's universal. Dave, Paige, and I had already learned to budget that sting into our adventures, regardless of country or continent. *Believe me, the trade-off is worth the trouble.* The real lesson was to remember that the world is filled with good people, to look for them, and to make sure I'm doing my part to be one of them.

South Africa

It felt good to be back in South Africa. For the first time in weeks, we recognized big chain shops around us. We relished the grocery stores and shopping malls. After Zimbabwe, we needed some comfort and familiarity, and, like a beacon of safety, McDonald's cholesterol-colored arches signaled 'Welcome Home.'

As we worked our way back to Johannesburg, we stayed a final couple of nights in the same campsite at the Blyde River Canyon. I couldn't remember the last morning we'd had without going through the hour-long process of packing up Bucky. For a brief couple of days, we had no place to be.

Conscious of the limited time that they had together, I encouraged Dave and Paige to take an all-day hike together without me. I kept thinking about how much I loved my own dad, and it was important to me that Dave and Paige get some special time alone together. Dave told me later that they'd had a great day out—that they'd really connected. Meanwhile, I'd luxuriated in my own time—reading fantasy fiction about assassins and fools, working on "The Best Seller," and compulsively twisting my hair into greasy, lanky clumps. The day was a much-needed triple win for our family.

Our time in the rental bakkie was coming to an end. The day soon arrived when we finally completed our enormous circle around the southern quarter of the African continent. Thirty-four days, 5,000 miles (8, 000 km), four countries, and two flat tires later, we said goodbye to our beloved Bucky in Jo-burg.

The Drakensberg Mountains – South Africa and Lesotho

Groups traveling together tend to sour, and Dave, Paige, and I had been in very close quarters for far too long. It had become a bit like eating powdered Kool-Aid drink mix directly from the packet. Our family dynamic needed some sugar and watering down, so we were all excited when Dave's older sister Gwen arrived from England to join us for the next leg of our journey.

We'd booked a six-day guided trek through the Drakensberg in South Africa. Bordering South Africa and Lesotho, the Drakensberg, or "dragon mountains," were one edge of the enormous Great Escarpment, a plateau that covered much of southern Africa. With peaks reaching over 3,000 m (9,800 ft) "The Berg" were the highest mountains in Africa south of Kilimanjaro, and a playground for hikers in the region. Over the course of six days, we planned to hike "The Northern Drakensberg Transverse." The difficulty was said to be "extreme," "for expert hikers," and "not for the fainthearted," but the views would be spectacular!

Our guides for the trip were two young men, Jack (23), a white South African and Solomon (20), a black South African and Zulu Tribesman. The small mountaineering company we'd hired for the trek was completely booked in those mid-winter weeks of the season. The more experienced owner, Rocky, who would be leading his own trip that week, assured us that these young guides were qualified, and that they had completed our hike a dozen times. So, we put our faith in these two men, and they didn't let us down.

Our first trekking day was a short one since the first half of it had been spent driving to the trailhead at Sentinel Peak. We were loaded to the gills with tents, camping stoves, food, and water. After the Fish River Canyon, this would be our family's second significant backcountry "trek," much different than the unencumbered hiking we'd done so much of in the past.

Gwendolyn had prepared for the trek. Of course, she was fit; being Gwen, she always kept herself lean and strong, and at 57, she made me look like a creampuff. However, for some strange reason, almost 30 years earlier, she'd developed a fear of heights just after her first pregnancy. Gwen, who had been skydiving in her youth, later struggled to hike to mountaintops, which hindered one of her favorite hobbies. So, with Gwen's trademark tenacity, in her mid-50s she signed up for a "Fear of Heights" course to attack it head-on. Since completing the course, she'd made huge progress, and had finished several perilous hikes with her son Derek in Europe. (After Africa, she would go on to hike throughout New Zealand and Nepal). Gwen felt ready to attempt the Northern Transverse, and we were happy to have her.

Gwen's mettle was quickly put to the test. On that first day, we soon came to an infamous feature called "The Chain Ladders." Attached to sheer vertical cliff sides were two sets of shifting metal ladders, which rocked on their chain fixtures with each step up the rungs. Each set of the ladders had about 50 rungs, but the first was a bit longer than the second. The overall ascent was approximately 50 m (160 ft), just over half the length of a football field!

Gwen wasn't the only one who struggled with heights. Paige also had to summon her courage. As we approached the ladders, they both began to fret and agonized before starting the ascent. We all watched Solomon go up first, to see how it was done. It took him almost a minute to reach the top. Sixty seconds was a long time to cling to the side of a cliff, especially while wearing a heavy trekking backpack.

I wasn't unsympathetic to Gwen or Paige's distress, but I knew if I paused too long I would be more likely to work myself into a panic. So, as soon as Solomon finished, I took a deep breath and immediately started climbing. I figured Dave, Jack, and Solomon could better support the others, and that the best thing I could do for our team was to handle myself. I stuck to a no-nonsense mantra that had served me well in times like these: *Screw this up, Amy, and you will DIE!* Actually, I just took it one step at a time and remembered to breathe, until I ran out of rungs.

Of course we all made it. I never doubted that we would. Paige was the next to reach the top, and Gwen soon followed, moving slow and steady. Dave came next, and Jack did the ladders twice, bringing up Gwen's backpack for her. I sat at the top, breathing with purpose to calm my nerves and exhaling with relief as each of the people I cared about made it to the top (including Jack, twice). It hadn't been easy for anyone, even for those of us not especially sensitive to heights. I had huge admiration for Paige and her "Auntie Gwendy" who had persevered through intense, completely justified fear.

Unfortunately, I'd later realize that my behavior hadn't communicated any of my concern. *So long, suckers,* I might as well have shouted and then spit down onto my struggling family below. On that African trip, sometimes I was better at climbing ladders than I was at building bridges.

On the top, the hiking was nice. The terrain was pleasant, solid and level, and the views were fantastic. I was having a wonderful day, until I realized that Gwen was ill.

Gwen hadn't mentioned, or perhaps hadn't yet realized, that she had a stomach virus. After the ladders, as we made our way across the plateau, it became clear that Gwen wasn't well. Being British and being Gwen, her intestines could have been dangling between her feet in the dirt, and she would only have said that she felt "a bit poorly." However, that afternoon, she actually had to stop a few times to vomit.

Jack was very concerned, but Gwen insisted that we continue. Dave had a medicine kit with tablets (stopper-uppers), and Solomon kindly took some weight from her pack. The group slowed its pace. I couldn't believe she'd done the ladders or this much of the trek in her condition. We headed to a winter trickle called Tugela Falls, which I was surprised to learn was the world's second tallest waterfall. We spent our first night camping there, hoping that Gwen would recover.

That night was a bitterly cold one. My entire vacation had seemed full of improbable superlatives, "The Brightest Stars," "The 2nd Hardest Physical Feat," "The Most Dramatic Sunrise," and "The Second Worst-ever Toilet." Perhaps I shouldn't have been surprised to experience "The Coldest I've Ever Been." It turned out that camping in the Drakensberg in July trumped Nepalese hiking huts in December, at least, according to this witch and her well-traveled tits. As soon as the sun went down, just after 6 p.m., the temperature dropped so low that I was forced into my down sleeping bag inside the tent. I spent 13 hours cocooned overnight before I felt warm enough to exit the next morning.

Fortunately, Gwen was feeling a bit better the next day, and she convinced Jack that she was able to push on. Astonishingly, she did. We took it slow and watched her closely, but she battled through it like a champion.

The next three days were gorgeous hiking days with fine weather and spectacular views, especially from The Amphitheatre. A massive horseshoe, the plateau stretched over three miles (5 km), with a sheer 4,000-foot drop (1,220 m) for its entire length. Dave, Paige, and I wiggled up to the edge, on our bellies, to stare down into what was widely regarded as "one of the most impressive cliff faces on Earth." Gwen passed. Fair enough.

Our group crossed back and forth, into and out of South Africa and Lesotho as we moved across the plateau. A big, quiet man, Solomon tended to walk far ahead of our group, leading the way. Jack became our human field guide. He told us, for example, that where the water flowed toward the cliffs was South Africa, and where it flowed inland was Lesotho. He was a charming guy, full of information and entertainment.

Easy to talk to and ever curious, Gwen teased out the details of Jack's life story. A relatively older (than Jack), well-traveled, outdoorswoman, Paige made him trip on his words. I hovered nearby, listening intensely and absorbing it all, as I processed Jack's tales behind my involuntary scowl. Meanwhile, Dave brought up the rear. He was in his happy place, hiking through mountains with his family of strong women.

On our fourth day, we reached a crossroads. Jack and Solomon had reservations about our itinerary. Because our family had struggled so much with The Ladders, Jack felt that we wouldn't be able to manage the Bell Traverse, which was a narrow path with sheer drops on either side. Our party already seemed "buggered," and what lay ahead would require a great deal of physical and psychological stamina. He and Solomon agreed that taking an alternative route down the mountain would be the best choice for our group. He gave us a moment to talk it over, but advised us against the original plan.

"I'd really like to go for it, but what do you all think?" Dave asked us.

Unfortunately, I spoke up next.

"Dave, if you asked us to, the three of us would follow you into hell," I proclaimed, and turned expectantly to Paige and Gwen.

I may have had a little too much mountain air.

Here's the thing. I write well, but I don't always talk too good. And when I'm hiking, I'm often writing in my mind. Sometimes sentences escape my mouth before they've finished cooking, and I can be disgustingly sentimental. That day in South Africa, my words aloud sounded much cornier than they had in my head.

Paige guffawed at my melodramatic, over-sugared presumption, and Gwen took a sudden, amused interest in her boots. Evidently, not only was I cheesy, I was also mistaken.

"Not me!" Paige wisecracked. "You two can go there (to hell) for your next holiday!"

CRACK!

Oh boy, it was a good one—a real zinger that would have made me howl if I'd watched it on a sitcom with a laugh track. However, by that point in our trip, Paige's biting humor ripped right through my very chafed, very thin skin. She hit a nerve.

I glared at my stepdaughter and sized her up. I felt pretty sure that I could take her ass.

And, if you were a smurf, your name would be Snarky, I mentally christened Paige.

Never mind that Snarky Smurf would have been my favorite character in the much-loved 1980s American cartoon about tiny, blue gnome-like creatures. It wasn't much of a burn, especially to a British child of the 90s. It's probably for the best that I didn't say my *cut-down* out loud.

Six weeks. Forgive us both, but our family had been on the road *for six long weeks.* We all deserved medals and pardons.

Auntie Gwendy jumped into the middle, before I could *smurf* that Smurf off a cliff.

"Dave, I'm really worried about Bell Traverse. I watched some videos before I left England, and they were frightening. Rather terrifying, to be honest. Paige and I talked it over in the tent last night. I'm sorry, but, I don't know if I can do this," Gwen apologized.

"Dad, I've given it a lot of thought, and I really don't want to do it either," Paige added.

It was clear that neither Paige nor Gwen felt comfortable with the crossing, but that they were reluctant to disappoint us by altering our plans.

Dave and I took a few moments alone to talk it over. I think that had Paige and Gwen not been with us, we probably would have gone for it. However, Jack and Solomon were the experts and had done this hike several times. They knew the capabilities of our group and what lay ahead. Plus, I had my own uncomfortable sensation, like when a close friend goes rooting around in your belly button.

"I don't have a good feeling about pushing them to do it. What do you think?"

"Yes. Considering all the factors, it isn't worth it," Dave agreed.

I suspected that Dave had also done mental "maths" and had run through some sort of quick military risk assessment. He had. He'd reevaluated our schedule and realized that, by forgoing the cliff walk, we could shave a day off our entire Drakensberg trek. This meant that instead of one, we'd have a full two days to recover before the four-day Otter Trail hike. I was again reminded that, while Dave's itinerary was brilliant, but *bladdy hell*, it was brutal!

Dave went to tell the others our verdict.

"Let's skip it. The extra day coupled with us not dying sounds good."

The descent the following morning would be a tough one. Because we'd decided to skip the Bell Transverse and Cathedral Peak, our alternative path down the mountain wasn't typically used by hikers. It was a steep, jagged cattle trail, with large boulders and big, scrambling drops. It ran straight down the deep gorge in front of us at a ridiculously steep angle. Just as I began to wonder if it was truly possible, a group of Basotho shepherds (from Lesotho) and their herd came along, to show us how it was done.

Half a dozen, wiry men on horseback nodded their heads in greeting as they approached. They were wrapped in thin, dust-darkened blankets, and, between them, they had perhaps 75 head of livestock. It was a mixture of mostly cows, and some sheep and goats, along with the four or five of the skinniest, happiest dogs I'd ever seen. Solomon went over for a conversation.

We learned that the shepherds planned to descend using the same, near vertical path. Looking down the gorge, I thought of those cheese-chasing competitions where people, usually men, hurled themselves downhill at high speed, toppling head over heels. I entertained myself with a G-rated version of the livestock going down this valley, in a similar way. I pictured sharp boulders, tumbling flying mooing Muppets, red confetti blood, and spaghetti intestines strewn all over. In real life, however, it would end up being just a disappointing coating of cow shit.

We decided to let the shepherds and their animals start first. I had no desire to compete for the path with the herd. The animals kept their heads down and into the ass of the next guy in line. Four legs seemed to help with balance, a bit like built-in walking poles. The cattle bounded down easily enough, not overthinking it.

Our turn was next.

The first hour of that eight-hour descent was more like rock climbing, or rather bouldering, but downhill. We used our arms as much as our legs, finding hand and foot holds, to navigate the drops. Sometimes we had to take off our backpacks in order to slip through narrow openings, but generally we just scraped down, often on our bottoms, through the rocky ledges. The path opened a bit after a couple of hours, but remained so steep that I was very glad for my walking sticks.

Our family was struggling. We all loved hiking, but trekking was proving to be *rough!* Carrying all the added weight of food and tents was breaking down our bodies, especially mine. It was soul-destroying to acknowledge that I probably wouldn't have the knees to do this sort of thing for much longer in my life. We struggled through a steep, painful, and even emotional downhill that final day.

Our one compensation was the breathtaking view, which could bring me back to gratitude when I needed it most.

Gwen, who was still not a hundred percent, pushed herself unnecessarily in an effort to stay far up front with Solomon. She hated feeling as though she might be holding the rest of us back, and I hated worrying that she was dehydrating up front, since I was carrying the water. (Her water bottle had broken, and we were sharing.) I couldn't catch up to her. She shouldn't have worried because the rest of us just shuffled along. As always, she was a trooper—probably the toughest woman I knew.

I was in the middle, battling blisters as well as knees. Despite purchasing the exact make of my old beloved hiking boots, and even doing a few short hikes to break them in, my feet weren't having it. My ring and pinky toes on each foot were raw, and both heels had blisters the size of 2-Euro coins that then ripped around the sides of my feet. The big toenail on my right foot would later go black and fall off, and my knees, which normally just whined, were screaming like baboons. Given the terrain and it being the fifth day of our hike, I moved very gingerly, obviously not doing well.

At one point, Paige, who was behind with Dave, made eye contact with me on a switchback.

"I'm sorry you're hurt," she offered.

I could tell she meant it.

"Thanks, Paige. Same goes for you," I replied.

I meant it back.

Actually, Paige was in a lot of pain, too. Like me, she looked close to tears at times. In her late twenties, Paige already had arthritis in her spine from an old snowboarding injury, and the trekking backpack certainly didn't help. Paige was a fighter, and perfectly capable of taking care of herself. However, I was glad for Dave to stay in the back with her, just for moral support, because she looked like a girl who needed her dad.

There, in the middle of our group on my own, I felt pretty broken down, and I started to feel homesick for my own father. I thought of my dad back home in Texas. At 71, he'd have never been able to join us on this kind of trip. But, he was always so proud of me and supportive of my adventures. I pictured him encouraging me, as he had done from the sidelines of so many of my childhood soccer games.

"Come on, Ame! You can do this," he would have said, lifting me up with his love and his belief in me.

"Thanks, Dad. I love you, too," I beamed to him from the other side of the world.

One hundred years later, we made it down. And, guess what? We passed through hell after all! It surprised me to learn that, in South Africa, once a person descends through every physical and emotional level of purgatory, at the bottom there's a hotel. And, in that hotel, I drank the best damn beer I've had in my whole damn life.

There were 48 hours before we were meant to start the next hike, the Otter Trail. Dave would never have chosen to plan the walks so close together, but our calendar was locked. Between the guide availability for the Drakensberg and reservations for the Otter Trail, which was a self-guided, hut-to-hut walk, the schedule was unforgiving.

After a hot shower and good night's sleep, I was still hobbling. My feet were mangled, and it felt like I'd sprained my right knee. As the clock ticked down, I had to accept that it would be foolish, and potentially dangerous, for me to attempt the next hike so soon. It was also telling that Dave didn't disagree. My body needed a break.

Alas, I let the three of them go without me, and got a hotel room alone for four nights. It was terrible, all that pizza and ice cream and Internet access. To say the least, I enjoyed having a quiet room to myself for the first time in weeks.

I used the time to take stock of all that we'd experienced: those stars above the Fish River Canyon, running down Dune 45, the honeymooning lions in Etosha, and Lily, paddling fearlessly through the Okavango Delta. I could still feel the thunder and mist of Victoria Falls, the electricity of that elephant charge, and my heart swelling in my chest, as I took in the view from the Drakensberg's Amphitheatre. We'd created so many memories that I never wanted to forget.

I didn't know then exactly how the rest of our journey would unfold, but I knew that our road trip was nearing its end. After the Otter Trail, Paige would take me for my first-ever bungee jump on the way to Cape Town, and later Dave and I would spend our seventh wedding anniversary drinking rich, red port in the vineyards. I couldn't yet picture how we'd board that plane to Nairobi or what it would feel like to summit Mount Kenya.

Alone in my hotel room, neither was I conscious of the difficult good-byes that lay ahead, first to Gwen, who we would visit again soon, nor later, more tearfully, to Paige in Zanzibar. We didn't know when we'd next see Dave's independent, brave, secretly sensitive girl. I knew I'd probably never be a maternal figure in Paige's life because neither of us really wanted that type of connection. Regardless, I'd be there for my stepdaughter if she ever needed me, and I still hoped that we could be friends. After all, as two strong females in a family, we were on a long, life journey together.

With four days on my own, I used my time wisely. I recorded my memories of our family vacation. I wrote my guts out. I already knew that our trip through Africa, let alone the Midlife Gap Year, was shaping up to be one of the best experiences of my life. This was only the beginning. Well, I mean, the beginning of my middle.

Still, make no mistake, surviving that *mother-luvin'* camping holiday took a whole lot of *mother-luvin'* work!

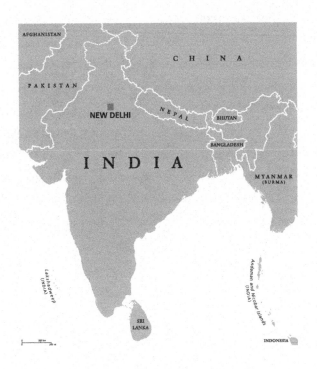

DRIVING IN BANGLADESH

Bangladesh, 2010—2013

The mile and a half distance from work to home can be walked in about 20 minutes or driven in an hour, depending on the day and time. We "rickshaw-it" when we can, but occasionally we need to drive. Any married couple in Dhaka will tell you how good this is for your relationship. If Dave drives, he regresses into a 16-year-old with anger management issues. I, in turn, morph into his mother—gasping, grabbing handles, and offering helpful suggestions. We do better when I drive, but where is the fun in that?

We wind, honk-honking through a video game of potholes, piles of sand, and carts laden with bricks and deceptively angled rebar. We avoid cycled school buses, bike-pulled cages filled with girls in Raggedy Ann, navy and white uniforms. We steer around tiny women sweeping endless dust with brooms of branch, between swerving rickshaws, and through a swirling river of people. Despite living in the world's most densely populated city, these pedestrians see no merit in looking before crossing. Vertebrae frozen, they teeter out in front of traffic at the last second, arms outstretched to hold up "the hand." All while gridlocked in marital bliss, we compete for every inch of road against countless other cars, driven by testosterone and its men.

SOUR PUSS

On Life, 1976–Present

Recently, I decided that I would try to look more pleasant in general.

You see, I tend to make people uncomfortable on accident. If I were an actor, I'm sure I'd be cast as a villain, in roles like *Woman with Machine Gun* or *Deranged School Bus Driver*. I'd make a great homocidal nurse, the sort of gal who slowly, over a period of several months, doses senior citizens with rat poison. My unsettling looks are a shame really, because although I have the face of a serial killer, inside I have the heart of a cocker spaniel.

I think it might have something to do with my brow line, a distinctive ledge that shadows my otherwise blank features into the illusion of Disapproval. On my forehead between my eyes are three permanent creases so deeply entrenched that they look like a miniature vagina—my facial vagina, my little "fag" /faj/. Years of lifeguarding and playing outdoor sports while squinting into the Texas sun formed this reproductive third eye. The fleshy crevice seems to swallow dirty seeds of oncoming self-doubt and give birth to paranoia in others. I *look like* I'm thinking,

"Would you like some parenting advice?"

Or

"Hurry up, dick munch. Move. Your. Truck!"

People tend to apologize to me in grocery store lines while I'm only thinking about whether or not to buy a candy bar.

I've spent a lot of time feeling misunderstood, so I've practiced "looking pleasant" on my husband. My features frozen into an agreeable expression, I'd wait for him to glance at me.

"Jeepers!" he'd cry out. "Don't do that to me!"

On other days, I'd ask, "How about now?" painting on yet another lovely visage.

"Oh dear, Madam," he'd sigh. "You look a bit like an imp."

One day, though, I found it. The perfect facial arrangement—easy and open—the kind of woman you'd ask where she got her shoes. Or the sort of lady you'd make chit-chat with at the park while your dogs ran around shitting in public and smelling each others' asses, as if it were all perfectly natural. To me, somehow it felt like tucking in my shirt—except it was my face.

"Sir! Quick! Look!" I gritted out.

As he turned to me, I swear angels sang, and he burst into a warm smile.

"My God, you look so lovely. What happened?"

For the next week, I tried out my new fake smile on passing strangers. Words cannot express how my experience of the world changed. Men in their twenties held doors for me. Smiling babies made me slimy offerings. One day a woman in the dressing room asked for my opinion.

"Oh, not that one," I fake-smiled.

"You are so right. What was I thinking?" she replied, and actually thanked me.

The thing is, all that "looking pleasant" was kind of exhausting. I mean, I'm pretty introverted, and smiling is inviting. Besides that, my face hurt. So after a few days, I let the whole thing drop—back into its naturally dour expression.

These days I save my fake smiles, and my real ones, for special occasions.

SWIFT JUSTICE

Ethiopia, 2014–2017

1

"Do you want to bring a rope? It can save your life," our guide Gebre asked.

I was skeptical. The list of additional charges was growing: church entrance fees, a guide, a guard for our parked car, a scout (*How was that different from a guide?*), and now a 'safety rope,' too.

Oh please, I thought. We were being nickel-and-dimed.

"Is a rope really necessary?" Dave asked, sharing my miserly exasperation.

Gebre took a moment to size us up.

"No, I think maybe you can do it. The climb is only a problem for old people and fat Americans," Gebre said, assuming that I was English like my more mature husband.

Dave and I scanned one another, each mentally questioning if our spouse fit Gebre's criterion. At the time Dave was 51, and my weight fluctuated. We made an unspoken agreement. There might have been a few extra years and pounds between us, but if "old" and "fat" were the yardsticks, then we decided we'd rather fall to our deaths than ask for the rope.

We finalized our plans, and Gebre squeezed into the backseat of our car, which was packed tight and full of trip trash from our two weeks on the road. Our next stop was Abuna Yemata Guh, a fifteenth-century, rock-hewn Ethiopian Orthodox church. It was hidden in a cliffside, so Gebre would show us the way.

Dust pelted against the back window as we flew down dirt roads. The landscape in Tigray, the northernmost of nine Ethiopian regions, reminded me a bit of New Mexico or Utah with its arid climate and red sandstone monuments. In this part of the world, however, the pinnacles and plateaus towered over fertile fields of hand-plowed crops, tiny villages of expert hand-cut stonework, and solitary six-year-old shepherds. I was surprised when we passed a train of camels. Gebre said they were merchants from the Afar Region, bringing salt to trade at the big market in Hawzien.

Throughout the thirty-minute drive, I chit-chatted with Gebre. He was a lean, small man, a new father in his mid-20s. Yet another good-looking Ethiopian, he had dark caramel-colored skin. Shallow, half-inch (12 mm) scars lined each of his temples and across his left eyebrow. Gebre, like many Tigrae, had undergone a cutting procedure in childhood that was believed to protect against future eye problems. These subtle, personalized notches also marked him as a man of the north.

On the way we pulled over to pick up a second man to guard our parked car. Soon after, we stopped in a field with a couple of other vehicles and got ready for the hour and a half hike up to the church. I was glad we were already acclimated since we'd been living in Addis Ababa, but at almost 7,000 feet (2,135 meters), we were careful to bring water and wear sunscreen on that deceptively pleasant day.

Before long, walking turned into climbing as we worked our way up a steep channel of boulders. We passed a family of five coming down on the way, and everyone struggled to find slots to squeeze by one another. An alarmingly quiet and serious group, even the 12-year-old boy looked rattled.

"Good luck," the father bid us ominously.

Soon after, we came to what *had to be* the notorious part, an almost vertical sandstone face with a series of natural hand grips and toeholds scattered along its surface. In front of us another group was slowly ascending. A scout spoke soothingly to a crying young woman who clung to the cliffside. Her friends and guide encouraged her from above. To her credit and everyone's relief, she eventually made it up. The poor girl wasn't old, overweight, or American but a rope might have helped.

Our turn was next.

Gebre introduced us to our scout Bahailu, a tall strong farmer in his 50s, dressed fittingly in camouflage. Bahailu instructed us to remove our hiking boots, and it was the right call because I immediately felt more secure, more connected to the sandstone. I went first. It was clear that Bahailu had a lifetime's familiarity with the route, using his few English words or, when those failed him, his body to guide my hands and feet to the correct places. Thankfully, I was numbed by adrenaline instead of panicked. It could have gone either way. When I finally reached the top, the drop was dizzying, and I needed a few moments to just sit and breathe. I couldn't bring myself to watch Dave ascend. However, with Bahailu's help, Dave made it, too.

As a final test, we teetered across a one-person-wide, several-person-long ledge that teased us with a sheer drop to certain death. Cut into the cliffside, it was there that the Ethiopian rock-hewn church Abuna Yemata Guh had hidden from the world since the sixth century, over 1,500 years. It was one of a handful of churches that wasn't found and burnt during a period of Islamic raids, so the inside hadn't been destroyed. The religious paintings inside were bright and crisp, impossibly young-looking to be so incredibly old.

It was worth the climb.

After a treacherous descent, our relieved hearts slowed as we put back on our boots. While Dave tipped the scout, I looked up to see two wiry Tigrayan grandmothers approaching. Easily in their 70s, both wore long cumbersome skirts and were wrapped in white shawls for church. Dark green dots and crosses were tattooed along their jawlines, necks, and foreheads, a decorative symbol of their Christian faith. Smiling and chatting, the ladies scrambled up the cliff face on their way to worship for the day. If they had any help up the cliff, it wasn't from Man.

After lunch, we made our way to our second church for the day, almost an hour's drive away on more rough country roads. Eventually, we headed toward a cluster of trees in the center of an open field. An empty tour bus was parked in the shade. Its dozing driver rested in the grass. Nearby, an eighty-year-old man and young granddaughter sat peacefully under a tree. Of the two, I wasn't sure who was minding whom. We pulled up behind the bus and parked.

"Oh, we forgot to get a guard for your car this time. Should we go back to town?" Gebre suddenly realized.

In hindsight, we were a novelty as two white people driving their own car, alone, around Northern Ethiopia, a first for Gebre, I'm sure. Other *ferenj* (foreigners) arrived in touring vans or jeeps, with their pre-packed lunches and drivers who guarded the vehicles while the tourists explored. Ordinarily, Gebre's role was to lead tourists to and around the rock-hewn churches, but he rarely, if ever, had been logistically responsible for a car. However, at the time we were paying Gebre to coordinate this experience for us, and I was quietly irritated that he hadn't thought of safeguarding our vehicle earlier, before driving *an hour* into the countryside. Dave and I hated the idea of going all the way back into town again, especially since we were on a schedule and still needed to check into a hotel for the night.

"Should we be worried?" I asked.

"Well, sometimes children play with the cars," Gebre hedged.

"Oh, well, that's no big deal," I said.

I shrugged at Dave, and he shrugged back in agreement. Kids didn't bother us. We were teachers, after all. We decided to take our chances. We put on more sunscreen, gathered up the camera and some water, and made our way up to the church.

We should have paid that grandfather and granddaughter to watch our car.

2

Unlike the first church, the one-and-a-half hour hike to Debre Tsion Abuna Abraham was easier, without "a tricky bit" that could kill us. We passed the tour group coming down as we reached the top, and I was relieved that we would have the place quietly to ourselves. There we found the unusual church, chiseled into rock. Part-building and part-cave, this sanctuary had unfortunately been found in history and burned by religious persecutors, but several faded paintings of St. Abraham, his lions, and the famed "Nine Syrian Monks" still decorated its walls.

As an added bonus, it was St. Mary's Day, and the resident priest had distilled a batch of local wine. He insisted we try it, and I weighed the consequences, knowing it'd give me the squirts to partake. In the end, I decided the trade-off was worthwhile, so I choked down just a couple sips of the cloudy yellow, cigarette-tasting brew.

Afterwards, we descended more quickly than we'd climbed, meaning, in total, we had been gone about three-and-a-half hours. I felt relieved that we should make it to our hotel before sunset. In the distance, I could see that the tour bus was gone, but our car was parked where we'd left it. A few kids milled around, nearby.

As we approached the car, I headed to the passenger side. Time slowed as I took in the scene before me. It was the shattered glass on the ground that caught my attention first. When I looked up, I noticed that the back passenger window had been smashed. Inside, glass covered the back seat, and our belongings were scattered. My mind stumbled into the realization that we'd been robbed.

"Dave. *Dave! Come here! The window is broken!*"

Hearing my distress, Dave rounded the car in disbelief. At the sight of the shattered window, he swore loud and long.

Meanwhile, a crowd of kids had started to form. At Dave's cursing, the children giggled with delight and discomfort. Several recognized the dirty English words that were learned behind schools, not inside them. In that moment, however, their laughter felt vicious so we turned on them. Like wounded dragons, we breathed fire and scattered little bodies into the fields.

Violated, raw, we picked through the glass and our possessions. It was clear that someone had climbed over the seats and dug through the far back of the SUV. Since we were between hotels, the thief had easily discovered our bags, which weren't well hidden under blankets. Several items were missing, including my purse with its wallet, my credit cards, and, worst of all, our passports.

By the time we reached a police outpost, it was late afternoon. The single officer at the village post, a corrugated metal shack, told us he'd make some calls and for us to come back tomorrow. Gebre suggested a nearby lodge where we could borrow the Internet to cancel our credit cards. The owner, Mario, was a Swiss *ferenj* who had lived in Ethiopia since 1991. His lodge was full, and we weren't able to stay there. Still, Mario was gracious and sympathetic. Like a respected grandfather, he reprimanded our guide.

"Gebre, these tourists trusted you to take care of them. You knew car theft was a problem in this area. This is your fault, too."

I appreciated that Mario thought Gebre should shoulder his share of the blame, and we *had* lost faith in our young guide. However, Dave and I were world travelers. We knew better. I was sick with myself for making such a colossally stupid, amateur decision. We'd even left our passports in the car. *Really, Amy? Idiot! Of all things, the passports!* This wasn't Gebre's fault. Ultimately, Dave and I had brought this on ourselves.

We had very little hope in general, as if returning the next day for police proceedings would be a waste of everyone's time. When we said as much to Mario, he disagreed, and called in his right hand man, his "fixer," a young Ethiopian named Tedros. Tedros knew Gebre from the guides' association in town, and he became a unifying bridge between us. Like Mario, Tedros also felt that returning to the police would be important. Inspiring confidence, he soothed us in excellent English that the criminals would be found, and took Dave's phone number. Tedros promised to follow up with the police, and said he would call us in the morning.

That night we drove an hour and a half in the dark back to Adigrat, a large town where we'd stayed the previous night. All the while, I prayed we wouldn't hit a person, someone's livestock, or be swallowed by one of the enormous potholes on the cheap, pitch-black roads. We didn't know where else to go, and Adigrat had Internet, an ATM machine (to empty my Ethiopian account with Dave's card), and a sheltered garage to park our smashed-open vehicle.

It was a long, painful night. The crime cut, the worry stung, but our self-punishment bruised most of all.

The next morning we made phone calls and closed our accounts. We "secured" the car window with plastic, mostly to keep the dust out. Tedros called to check in with us, and to make sure we were coming.

"Should we even go back? You know we'll just be a spectacle," I asked Dave when he got off the phone.

"You may be right, but if Mario feels we should be there, then I think we should go."

So back we went, but I wasn't optimistic. In Hawzien, on our way to the police station, we picked up Gebre and Tedros. From there we drove silently into the countryside together. This time, instead of reminding me of home, the pinnacles and plateaus on the horizon were forbidding. *You don't belong here,* they whispered.

We arrived at the police station about 11 a.m., and the place was busy. Almost a dozen men were gathered outside the building. The guides hopped out and greeted men with Ethiopian handshakes that included double-shoulder bumps, a holdover from the days of carrying rifles. They got information while we parked. When Tedros made it back to us with an update, we were surprised to learn that a few suspects had already been rounded up, five teenage boys from the local area.

"How did they find them all so quickly?" I asked Tedros.

He wavered, and then opted for honesty with a shrug.

"Well, they just got all the bad boys from the village and hit them with sticks until someone told the truth."

At the police station, we were escorted into a small concrete building where we, and then Gebre, were questioned by investigators. Three men took notes as we reported what had happened. All the while, Tedros interpreted the questions and our answers, but he skipped much of the internal talk among men. Dave and I were lost, putting our hope into a foreign system we did not understand. The outcome was no longer in our hands.

At one point, I was asked to list all the items that had been taken. This included my purse, several credit cards and various identification cards, a scarf, my cell phone, car and house keys, some wet wipes and hand sanitizer, a pair of broken black shoes, $50, and less than $10 in Ethiopian birr. Worst of all, our passports had been stolen.

"Are you *sure* there isn't anything else?" one man seemingly led.

We couldn't be certain. Maybe some clothing?

After our interviews, five different "bad boys" were pulled into the room, one by one, and interrogated in front of us. They looked to range in age from about 12 to 16. No one remembered to interpret for us, and it seemed better not to interrupt the Ethiopian process. Dave and I were left to draw our own conclusions based on body language. Some of the boys looked remorseful. One was teary. Others were cocky. They were all scared.

I felt torn and went numb.

As the interrogation ended, Tedros explained that during the questioning, two of the boys confessed to everything. They admitted to smashing the window with rocks and stealing my purse and a few other items. The thieves had waited for the tourist bus to leave, and they then had a 45-minute window to commit the crime before we returned. There had been three key players involved: a window smasher, a lookout, and a burglar who climbed into our car. Everyone had been rounded up, except for the last boy. He had taken the bus to the larger town, Wukro, to exchange the American dollars for Ethiopian birr at a bank.

At the police station, The Lookout said they'd dumped my purse and most of its contents, which included the cards, into a deep puddle behind a stone wall, not far from the incident. Dave and I thought it was strange that the boys hadn't kept the credit cards too, but Tedros explained that the thieves, poor farm boys, would not have been able to explain having credit cards in the first place. And, they wouldn't have known how to use them for online purchases. It was a sad reality, but in this instance it worked in our favor. Best of all small mercies, The Lookout said he could take us back to my belongings.

The policemen mobilized into action. With one of the few cars on hand, Dave and I were asked to drive Tedros, two police officers, and two of the boys to the scene. We didn't want the boys in our car, but it seemed petulant to refuse. Thieves turned passengers, everyone got a lift as we raced after the cloud of dust left by the speeding police truck. Dave struggled to keep up.

Several bumpy, dusty minutes later we reached a field, where we got out and hiked to a rock wall in its center. Behind it, we found my soggy purse in a puddle, near the top of a deep muddy hole. Most of its contents were scattered on the ground. Little cotton parachutes littered the area; the soaked, bloated tampons had confused the boys first and now they bewildered the policemen. (Pads were common, but even among my Ethiopian friends in Addis Ababa, big-city women with Master's degrees, tampons could be a disturbing mystery). That day in Tigray, a dozen rural men inadvertently considered my womanly privates, my bleeding and not-so-different body. We were all embarrassed, but I held my head high and dared them to look me in the eyes.

I was relieved when we found the credit cards, although we'd already had them canceled. We also found my scarf and a few other random items from my purse. One agreeable man drew the short straw; he lay on the ground and then stuck his arm into the muddy hole, up to his shoulder, to search for more sunken items. However, he didn't find the money, my cell phone, or our passports.

As two young men caught up in the excitement of a real police investigation, and yet still somehow our tour guides, Tedros and Gebre often forgot to interpret for us. We repeatedly had to ask them, "Where are we going?" and "What's happening now?" Like novice dance partners, we followed our leaders, but each step along the way was a surprise to us, a clumsy lurch to understand and keep up. Spinning through the Tigrayan countryside, as the events continued to unfold that day, we hung on for dear life.

From the stone wall, we followed the police cars to the boys' homes to collect our stolen things. The Lookout hadn't taken anything, other than 100 birr, $5 USD, for his role. The Window Smasher, however, went into his home to collect our property: a broken pair of my shoes (that he'd already mended with a needle and string), one of Dave's t-shirts, a thermometer from our medicine kit, and two pairs of Dave's dingy old underwear. They would have been twice the boy's size.

Dave joked, "What on Earth would he want with a middle-aged man's underpants?"

It was only a little bit funny, but I was careful not to laugh, for fear my amusement would be misconstrued. I knew, for better or worse, we represented all white people. We also knew the boy stole Dave's underwear because he or someone he knew could use them, and his need was heartbreaking. In another context, I would have bought him a dozen new pairs. However, the boy had smashed out our car window to take what was ours. Caught in a terrible situation, Dave and I pocketed that small thread of humor, the stolen underwear.

Finally, we found ourselves at the last boy's house, The Burglar who had climbed into our car, who was now in Wukro. We hoped to find our money, my cell phone, and the passports. Instead, we found the boy's father, mother, and siblings. The family was cooperative. In Ethiopian law, if rights existed to prevent such a search, then neither the uneducated parents nor we ignorant foreigners understood those legalities. I wondered if the stoic parents were just giving their son the benefit of the doubt as the authorities combed through their humble but tidy Tigrayan home. The police found nothing.

3

By 5 p.m. that afternoon the third boy still hadn't come home from the city. We'd returned to the police station after a long day, and by this point Dave and I hadn't eaten in almost 30 hours. The police decided we should regroup the following day, and we prepared to find a hotel. As Dave and I resigned ourselves to another day of uncertainty, there was a sudden flurry of activity.

"The boy called a friend! He's on the bus, on his way back. Come on!" exclaimed Tedros.

Our crew of two foreigners, two tour guides, two thieves, and a policeman piled back into our SUV and took off. Then, for the first and probably only time in my life, I found myself in an actual police chase!

The adrenaline in the air left a metallic taste on my tongue. Racing dangerously over rutted roads, we struggled to keep up with the lawmen. We soon gained on a lumbering city bus in the distance. As we approached, the police truck honked and swerved, shouting at the bus driver to pull over. Cops jumped from the back of the truck, and beat on the side of the bus for it to open. Officers pushed inside to search for the boy among the passengers, but he'd already gotten off.

Before I had a chance to get disappointed, the police truck was off again. This time we raced to a friend's house, and officers flooded the scene to apprehend the third boy. Caught up in the moment, our tour guides jumped out of our car and raided the house like policemen. Meanwhile, the cop who was riding in our car grabbed The Lookout, and raced with him into the mix. It was his job to keep the boys separated, so their stories wouldn't change.

As all hell broke loose outside, Dave and I looked up in the quiet to realize we were sitting, alone in the car, with the boy who had smashed open our car window.

We both turned to face the little punk.

I suspect that very few victims of a crime in the Western world get the chance to be alone with their perpetrators, after the fact. It's probably for the best. For me, the chance to confront the boy brought forth a troubling mixture of feelings. I was more grieved than gratified, especially as I watched my husband's anger grow.

"Look at me, Boy," Dave growled.

He proceeded to let his fury loose, verbally. I had never seen Dave so mad, so close to losing control. It didn't matter that he and the boy spoke different languages. Understanding was clear. Eventually, more scared than sorry, the thief was reduced to tears. I didn't want to undermine my partner, but I knew this needed to stop.

"Dave, let's take a break," I tiptoed.

It took a moment, but my voice brought him back. Dave shook his eyes clear. We left the boy crying inside our car, sitting on a blanket that couldn't protect him from the remnants of shattered glass.

Outside of the car, the final boy had been pulled from his friend's home, and the police and our guides were questioning him. A typical teenager, the boy's first response was to mouth off. Evidently, he'd made a disrespectful crack because Detective Tedros, who was enjoying a recent self-promotion from Tour Guide, didn't like the boy's tone. He reeled back and backhanded the boy, once, across the face. It got everyone's attention, and the cops stepped in to let Tedros cool off.

It didn't take long for the boy to confess. In the 10-minute drive back to the police station, the boy admitted to everything and agreed to hand over our passports. They were hidden in his home. The police hadn't found them in their earlier search. Since we were already in the car, we stopped by his house on the way back. There, the boy collected our things—both passports, the cellphone, and the remaining cash. He had spent less than $5.

We had everything back. I was weak with relief.

Nearby, his father wept silently in the grass.

Over the course of the next three days the police reports, painstakingly written with pen and carbon paper, were collected and filed into thick binders that lined the walls. It was 2014. The local tourist board sent over an interpreter, Hailu, who took care of us in the days that followed. A well-educated man who had gone to university in Addis, Hailu was incredibly supportive, giving up two days of his time to escort us through a foreign legal process. The community, including police, militia, the tourist board, and prosecutors, all rallied to process our case as quickly as possible, in days instead of weeks. Car theft had been a growing problem in the area, and even the Minister of Tourism's car had been broken into while parked in the countryside. The community was eager to prosecute the boys, and to make an example out of our case. Even the local press arrived to cover our story. The momentum swept us away.

The Ethiopians we met were horrified and disgraced that this had happened to guests in their country. Strangers in cafés were sympathetic and apologetic. Lovely people surrounded us, and their kindness was a balm for our sufferers' cynicism. We were reminded that Ethiopia was full of trustworthy, generous people, and that there are foolish boys all over the world.

Humor doesn't always translate across cultures, but more than once over the course of our three days together, Hailu and I laughed to tears at the thought of Dave's dingy old underpants being presented as evidence in court. Dave faked outrage to add to our pleasure, but he chuckled, too. When our court date came, and two pairs of stretched-out, threadbare, yellowing underwear were presented to the courtroom, I was careful not to make eye contact with Hailu, as I felt his body quietly shaking, tittering next to mine.

At the trial, all three boys admitted to everything, and their story never changed. School dropouts, they already had a reputation for trouble in the community. As was common in the area, one of the boys didn't know his birthday. They were 15, about 16, and 17 years old. The boys didn't appear to have legal representation, and no one came to support them in court. A brown judge in a white wig sentenced all three boys to two years and ten months in prison. Based on their bravado afterwards, I didn't think the boys grasped the full consequences of their actions. Yet.

My heart hurt for the parents and their lost sons.

The keys were never found. We suspected they sank to the bottom of that deep puddle. It took ages to replace the glass in our back passenger window. The car stayed safely in our garage in the meantime, taped up with plastic. We took taxis or rode with friends instead, for six months. When Dave finally made it back to Europe on a professional training, he returned with a car window in his checked luggage, and later installed it himself. We finangled the situation so that our job ended up paying for the flight. We paid for the window.

I've spent years replaying those events in my mind. In the US or the UK, I doubt the thieves would have ever been apprehended. Given the systems of law in our own countries, at home, Dave and I would have kissed our belongings goodbye. A dear friend from Addis Ababa tells me that the same would have been true in Ethiopia's capital city. In rural Tigray, however, justice had been swift. Unfortunately, our retribution has never felt very good.

THE WATER FIGHT

Thailand, 2008–2010

I lived in Chiang Mai, Thailand, for two years. It was my first overseas post with Dave, and also where we officially became a couple. The country holds a special place in our hearts, and years after having left, we still love it and miss it like home. With a relaxed cultural vibe underpinned by Buddhist acceptance and compassion, a favorable exchange rate, English everywhere, super-cheap massages, delicious local street food, a warm climate, beaches, and excellent medical facilities, it's no wonder that so many Westerners choose to retire in Thailand. It's a fantastic place to live and grow older.

Over time I have come to realize that stereotyping is irresponsible. They are bastardizations born from the semen of truth. However, back when I lived in Thailand, to me, there seemed to be a disproportionately high number of aging weird white guys with beautiful young Thai women. Mind you, it was certainly *not* the norm, but those relationships did exist. Of those, not all mixed-aged couples were young bar girls and sad old perverts, each exploiting the other. I met several couples with big age differences who deeply loved their children and each other. Living in Thailand, I was reminded that there are many versions of family. *And besides, with a weird white English husband who was 14 years my senior, honestly, who was I to judge?* Maybe that was part of why we loved that country so much; we fit right in.

I track my adulthood by the countries I've called home. Before Dave, I lived in Germany and South Korea. He joined me in Thailand, and we've been together ever since—in Bangladesh, England, Ethiopia, and beyond. Over a decade of my life has passed overseas.

Sometimes I forget that those years also mark my age. In Garmisch-Partenkirchen, I was in my late 20s. On Jeju Island, I turned 31. I spent my early 30s in Chiang Mai, my mid-30s in Dhaka, and I turned 37 in Brighton. I finished my fourth decade in Addis Ababa. I turned 41 between homes, during our year off.

Good God. It's really happening like they said it would. I'm starting to get old. Well, at least I know where the time has gone.

Of all the places I've lived so far, Thailand has my favorite holidays, in particular Loi Krothong and Songkran.

Loi Krothong usually takes place in November, on a breezy fall evening. It's a Full Moon Festival of floating lanterns, both in the water and sky. Huge crowds gather to release large, parade-like floats and small, homemade boats, made from bread and banana leaves, into the local waterways. It's said to honor the water spirits.

My favorite Loi Krothong celebration happens in the north, outside of Chiang Mai, where tens of thousands of paper lanterns are simultaneously freed into the sky. It creates a surreal scene of fiery jellyfish, swirling up into the heavens. Back in 2008, I released my lanterns with love for my family and friends, but tradition says it's to symbolize letting go of anger. Either way, it's a magical night to release negativity and build positive karma.

Thai New Year, or Songkran, is another incredible celebration. A week-long, country-wide water fight, no one is left dry (well, except for elderly people dressed to head to the Temple. It would take a cold-hearted jerk to splash Grannie on her way to church—something inevitably done by some dumb, drunk tourist). People line the streets with buckets of freezing water and water guns, spraying anyone who passes. Small children soak accommodating adults who walk a little slower to get hit and then squeal with feigned outrage. Basically, if you're a local, the water fight is a blast the first day, fun for about an hour the second day, and really annoying the third day. Imagine a drenched loaf of bread on your way home from a quick trip to the shop. Tourists, however, love it.

An added thrill is that, actually, Songkran is pretty dangerous. Local newspapers keep a running death toll for the week. Things happen, like ice-cold water gets thrown into the faces of moped drivers who lose control and crash. Or, drunken people chase each other into streets in front of traffic. It's a shame that so many people get injured.

A Thai friend warned me to cover my ears during Songkran. She said one of the most common injuries is a burst eardrum. To make matters worse, the water is often from the old moat, so it can be incredibly dirty. Eye injuries and infections are also typical. She also said that young people, especially young foreigners on holiday, have a tendency to take things too far. The spirit of Songkran is supposed to be fun, a light-hearted way to wash away the evil deeds and to enjoy friends. It's meant to be a day of laughter, but often things escalate into obnoxious and then dangerous situations.

Taking the good with the bad, I still think Thai New Year is one of the best holidays in the world.

As I get older, I get softer (and I don't just mean my body). Through the years, I've prided myself on things like having received a Division I soccer scholarship, carrying all my own gear up to Everest Base Camp, tent camping for 50 consecutive days, or on having stayed in $10-a-night Thai beach huts, lice included, back when those huts actually existed.

As time goes on, I've come to realize two things: A) Actually, no one gives a shit. And B) Those things weren't all that pleasant. Of course, there was merit in having pushed myself, but I'm not sure how much I actually *liked* it. Let's be honest, "bragging rights" aren't worth much, and they bore people. These days I'd rather enjoy myself than prove myself, so I'm learning to cultivate my own happiness.

In my late 30s, I instituted a new personal rule: in Southeast Asia, my hotel rooms could cost my age. For example, if I were 38 years old, my hotel room could cost $38, which at that time got me a pretty nice place with my own bathroom. The policy wasn't especially frugal or bohemian of me, but my relentless inner critic would no longer be allowed to ridicule me for this pampering. (*I finally just named that personal self-terrorist "Astrid," after a terrible woman I would meet, years later on a rafting trip in Tasmania*). The new rule has been working out well for me, and turning 40 was nice because I graduated to "mid-range" hotels. This isn't to say I have always stuck to the price range, especially if I'm not in Southeast Asia. However, concessions like my hotel rule have helped me to live with Astrid, and to love her anyway.

In recent years, I forced Astrid to start meditating with me. We're still working on discipline, but the mindfulness is helping us both. I'm learning to have more compassion for myself and her. It's funny how Astrid's gravelly voice mellows as we get older.

Don't trip on your tits, Grandma! I mean, just give it your best shot, Toots.

Thanks, Astrid.

In April of 2012, Dave and I had already moved to Bangladesh, but we returned to Thailand on vacation. (We stayed in a luxury hotel—one that cost Dave's age!) It happened to be the 2555 Thai New Year, according to the Buddhist calendar. We didn't know Bangkok well, and since it was Songkran, we headed to a place where we knew *something* ought to be happening: Khao San Road. To say the least, it wasn't our best-ever idea, and it set the scene for one of my most dazzlingly immature performances.

Khao San Road was a 20-year-old backpacker's paradise. A tourist trap, it was not the Thailand we had grown to love. Instead, it reeked of patchouli and one-night stands. With cheap hostels, loud bars, Internet cafés, and bikini vendors, the area was Bangkok's hub for young travellers.

That night the tuk-tuk driver dropped us within a few blocks of Khao San, to the edge of the traffic and crowds. From there we followed the pumping music and young, wet, drunk people, who eyed our dry clothes with mischief.

"You're so dry!" one girl sang out and stumbled. "Not for looooong!"

All around us, water flew through the air, and people smeared each other with a grimy white paste (for good luck). On the fringes, gap-year kids chugged beer, danced, made out, stumbled, and vomited. Good old-fashioned fun, if you were under 25.

By the time Dave and I actually reached the main street, we were already soaked. We arranged a meeting point in case we got separated. That in itself probably showed our age, since younger people carried cell phones and could easily sort out getting lost. Like cave people, Dave and I found a big rock, and planned to return to it if we lost one another.

Meanwhile, in that crowd, I felt old old. At 34, I might have been able to pass in low lighting, but Dave at 48, bless his calcifying heart, just looked like someone's dad lost at a frat party. I felt sure we gave off the scent of mothballs as the youngsters brushed against our thin, wrinkling skins. I worried that one of us might slip in all that water and break a hip.

At the start of the main street, I grabbed a handful of Dave's shirttail as we got sucked into the heaving mass of people. There was no easy way to turn back, so we took a deep breath and committed to the half-mile stretch. Tabletops lined the side of the road, most offering a 3-Beer-Deal. To fortify ourselves, Dave and I split one deal, and then another, in rapid succession. Like a basketball player, I used my body to box-out the crowd, creating space for Dave to make our purchases.

As we made our way through the madness, I noticed a guy with an enormous super-shooter up ahead to my left. Remembering my friend's warning about burst eardrums, I covered my ear with my hand as we passed, just in case. It was a good thing I did because an instant later an ice-cold stream of water shot directly into the back of my hand, precisely, as if aimed for my ear. I kept walking and felt another long cold burst beat into the back of my head. *WTF.* It didn't feel playful, and it certainly wasn't incidental; it felt mean.

I turned to look at the shooter. He was in his early 20s, a big guy in a rugby jersey. I felt sure he was very drunk.

I raised an angry eyebrow at him, and mouthed the word, "Ouch."

He and his friends burst out laughing. Then, in reply, he emptied his enormous super soaker directly into my face. It took about 20 stinging seconds because I didn't turn away. He was only about 20 feet (6 meters) away.

When the stream finally fizzled out, I wiped my eyes and shouted, "You are hurting people, you dick!"

He and his inebriated buddies found my outrage absolutely hilarious.

Looking back, I'm sure I was just one of dozens of people he targeted that night—another casualty of his drunken, thoughtless, random "fun." Because he was aiming for ears, I wouldn't be at all surprised if he burst more than one eardrum that night. Regardless, he hit my insecurity like a bull's-eye. I felt like I'd been singled out because of my age.

Mind you, as scrappy as I am in my own head, I hate conflict. I've never been in a physical fight with anyone (except for my older sister and her prehensile, pinching toes—which doesn't count). But, that night something inside me snapped.

I thought to myself, *Okay, you little jerk. If you think I'm just an old auntie, then I'll act like one.*

So, fueled with liquid courage, I charged over to slap some sense into him. I reeled back and smacked him once, hard, right across his baby face.

POP!

It stunned us both.

My ancient reflexes didn't fail me, and I recovered first. Horrified, I turned, dove, and was swallowed by the swirling mass of bodies. Thankfully, Dave was up ahead and missed the whole ugly scene, including what would surely have required his noble-but-geriatric attempt to defend me from a pack of 22-year-old rugby players.

In hindsight, any wisdom that I had developed with age melted away on Thai New Year's Eve 2055. My maturity and I disappeared that night, lost into a wrinkle in the crowd. At the time, thirty-four seemed old to me, but clearly Astrid and I still had some growing up to do.

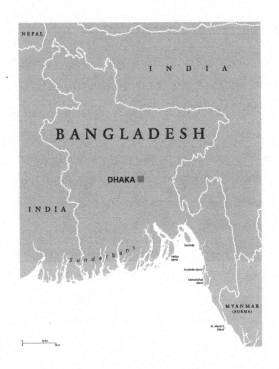

NO LAND'S MAN

Bangladesh, 2010–2013

In October of 2011, our second of three years living in Dhaka, Bangladesh, Dave and I took a trip 115 miles northeast to a little town in the hills. It was an area known for its tea gardens.

In the most densely populated city in the world at the time, it was no surprise that the train station in Dhaka was full of people. Grubby young boys ran across the tracks collecting plastic bottles to exchange for money. They dashed by a shirtless beggar who knelt on a piece of cardboard. His brown skin was entirely covered in rough bumpy nodules, and people without much of their own still stopped to give to a suffering man. Meanwhile, men dressed in white caps and white tunics stood together, chatting outside a steaming tea stall after the midday prayers. Their dutiful wives and daughters gathered in groups, like colorful bouquets in their bright saris. From outside the station, a line of rickshaw-wallahs touted for their next fare.

I knew we'd be travelling to a smaller town so I had dressed in local clothing, a red and brown salwar kameez—an incredibly comfortable outfit consisting of loose pajama-like pants, a long tunic top, and a scarf draped backwards across my chest and trailing over each shoulder; "Boob-a-flage," a friend had called it. I wanted to respect the culture, and I foolishly hoped it would help me to blend in.

As we waited, a crowd of about 20 people formed a semicircle to look at us. A few took pictures with their cell phones, but we didn't pose. In Bangladesh it wasn't considered rude to stare, and having lived there for a year already, Dave and I were accustomed to intense curiosity. I was never comfortable with it, but there at the train station, far from the comfort of the Diplomatic Zone where foreigners were more common, the attention seemed somehow less friendly. The crowd shamelessly took in Dave and me, his woman. I'm sure my gently lined, 30-something face looked worried. My freckled, outlandishly un-pierced nostrils shifted uneasily with each nervous breath.

I felt like an attraction at an old freak show, completely objectified. I imagined the people to be saying, "Is that his wife? It's dressed like a woman, but it's bigger than most men. Why would he let her cut her hair so short? And where are their children? Maybe she's like a mule and can't have them." In retrospect, their speculations probably weren't so ruthless, but that day uncertainty boiled within me. To relieve some pressure, I tried to smile at a little girl, but I only scared her into the folds of her mother's skirt. I understood her impulse, and stepped closer to Dave for similar reassurance.

Twenty minutes late and right on Bangladeshi time, the train pulled into the station. We knew that traditional Bangladeshi numbers, the numerals, weren't written as Western numbers, but we'd assumed the train cars would have both. They didn't. Precious seconds ticked by as we tried to match the squiggly symbols on our ticket to markings on the cars. All the while, masses of people piled into and climbed onto the train. We began to panic.

"Dave, the train is about to leave without us! Just ask someone for help!" I pleaded.

He nodded his head and scanned the crowd for any friendly face. As he approached his choice, Dave's volume rose as it often did in those early days when he spoke to non-English speakers in English. Plus, he was stressed and only complicated his request with confusing pleasantries.

"PARDON ME. COULD YOU PLEASE TELL ME WHERE TO FIND OUR SEATS?"

The Bangladeshi man didn't speak English, or to be more accurate, Dave (and I) didn't speak Bangla. Mercifully, the stranger was hospitable and overwhelmingly generous to us, like so many of the Bangladeshis we encountered during our time in the country. A game like charades unfolded, with pantomime and a shouting gallery of helpers. Soon the crowd figured out that we couldn't find our train car. The man left his family in a shot, and ushered us, running, to our carriage at the other end of the crowded platform. He helped us find our train car within seconds of it leaving.

"Dhonnobad! Dhonnobad!" we thanked him profusely with the insufficient words we had.

I hoped he would find his family again, in time to say goodbye.

Earlier that week, Dave had gone to the train station to purchase our tickets, an errand that turned into an adventure when the managers invited him into the main engineering room for tea and to learn about the trains. He had been told by friends to buy "first-class tickets" which, we later realized, would have put us into a private, air-conditioned compartment. Luckily, there was a miscommunication, and we ended up in one of the main cars, with open windows and surrounded by local people. To us, they were actually much better seats because we wanted to experience the culture. With the monsoon season behind us, the weather was gorgeous, and the breeze through the windows would be nice.

Inside the train, we found a family of five crammed into our two seats, but more protective onlookers cleared them out of our chairs, barking reprimands at the women and their children. The trip would take several hours, so we smiled apologetically and squeezed into our window seats, facing each other. Bodies pressed against mine, I stuck my head out the window to make more room for everyone, but also for a break from the onion air, the natural odor of a great pile of humanity.

Below me, braying vendors sold bananas, spicy puffed rice mixes in newspaper cones, and bags of popcorn from stockpiles which they balanced on their heads. Above me, from the roof, a man bought a bottle of water, lying down on his belly to make the exchange. The whistle blew as the train pulled away from the station. Shortly after, a train attendant muscled through our car, pushing those in the wrong place down the train, like a fist squeezing a tube of toothpaste with the cap still on.

Outside of Dhaka, Bangladesh was beautiful. The dirty buildings crumbled away leaving a marbled landscape of bright greens and browns. A land with criss-crossing rivers and the largest river delta in the world, the country was also home to freshwater river dolphins, bright blue and orange kingfishers, and Bengal tigers, which were surprisingly good swimmers. On our way to the tea capital, we crossed over several rusted steel bridges and gently chugged up, up, up into emerald hills.

When we arrived and exited the train station, street children immediately surrounded us.

"Dave, watch your wallet!" I shouted.

Having toughened during the previous year in Dhaka, we picked up speed to lose them. We zigzagged for a couple of blocks, making sharp cuts between taxis, carts, and rickshaws. One determined little girl, perhaps nine years old, locked onto my arm and put on an exaggerated mask of desperation. From begging, she'd downshifted into harassment. She and I both knew the difference.

"Let go. You're hurting me," I snarled.

Eventually, I tried to pry the girl's hand from my arm. Onlookers nearby scolded her with harsh words, and she finally released me. A lifetime's experience had taught this tenacious little girl to keep trying. Often enough, "no" eventually meant "yes," especially with the white foreigners. She scowled at me and walked away, leaving me feeling both outraged and ashamed, an emotional polarity to which I had sadly grown accustomed.

Eventually we found a CNG, a motorized tin-can taxi, named for its fuel—Compressed Natural Gas. I could tell it was rare for the driver to have a foreign couple in the back. He stopped three times to ask directions to our "upscale" accommodation, bamboo huts in an eco-lodge outside of town.

For me, the hardest part of our three years in Bangladesh was self-preserving in the face of bottomless need. In a developing country where foreign aid was making astounding differences, the locals had learned that outsiders brought opportunities, money, and help. Daily, for three years, Dave and I were bombarded by beggars, desperate families, staff, charlatans, entrepreneurs, and even well-intentioned humanitarians with requests to share our school teacher's "wealth." The expectation for charity was compounded by the kindhearted, almsgiving Muslim culture, in which the rich *should* help the poor, especially when the government did so little for its people. With unending pressure to *give, help, save,* my imperfect reactions fluctuated between compassion, heartache, outrage, guilt, and a sort of resigned bravado about "sustainability." I struggled to find the right balance.

Earlier that year, I asked a Bangladeshi-American friend Sonia for advice because I was finding it so difficult as an expat living in Bangladesh. Sonia was born in Bangladesh, but she had American citizenship, too. As a teenager, her family immigrated to Texas, where she grew up and worked as a high school biology teacher. She went on to get a Ph.D. in Science Education. At that time, she'd taken a teaching post back in Bangladesh, and we were teaching colleagues. Sonia said, "Amy, that's a tough one. There is no simple answer because most people don't need to be 'saved'; they need opportunities. Some of my friends pass out food, instead of money. Other people choose to *only* support grandmothers or *only* help people with disabilities. I have another friend who allots 100 taka per day (the equivalent of $3) to give to beggars on the street. My family volunteers through our mosque, but you have to find what feels right for you. Amy, I encourage you to do research, but don't let it paralyze you into doing nothing. Be sure to choose *something* because you can make a difference to someone each day."

Later during my posting, Sonia challenged me to think about my use of the word "expat" (expatriate), pointing out that it's a glamorous word, usually reserved for privileged, white people *who drink gin and tonics at sunset*. As a head-covering, brown woman who was a teacher just like me (except that she was trilingual, more highly educated, and more experienced), Sonia was usually referred to as "an immigrant," a "migrant worker" or "a foreign national." Meanwhile, I got to be an "expat." She argued that the word stank of colonialism.

To be honest, my first reaction was defensiveness. Most of the "expats" I knew were teachers (*even teachers of color!*) and people working in development—good folks trying to make a positive difference in the world. We, of all people, didn't deserve to be shamed. *Hell yeah, we drank gin-and-tonics, after a long day of teaching children in* (arguably) *the world's toughest place to live!*

However, by then I'd also learned that the things that piss me off in life usually mean I need to take a peek inside. I knew that Sonia had a point, and she kindly articulated it, too—neither of which was her responsibility. Once I cooled off, I accepted that discrimination (be it based on race, class, religion, or some other factor) can seem hidden to and within those of us who are sincerely trying to get it right. Was the word "expat" a blind spot of mine?

Oh God, did I have others? In order to emotionally survive Bangladesh, my rich white skin had to thicken without becoming calloused.

The next morning we asked the hotel owners if they knew of a place where we could rent bikes. We'd heard this was the best way to explore the tea plantations. A quick phone call was made, and soon an enterprising boy arrived with his little brother and two rusty old bicycles. The older brother offered us a test ride. As the deal unfolded, it dawned on me that these crummy bikes weren't your typical "rental" bikes; they were the boys' personal bikes. For us, that sealed the deal, and we happily paid their asking price, about $5 for the entire day.

We spent that warm morning riding around the area, eventually making our way to the tea plantation down the road. Concrete streets were lined with houses of corrugated metal, wet green fields, and bright but dingy saris drying on clotheslines. The shy smiling faces of women and children peeked out of door frames. The attention here felt different, more innocent and kind. Like any place in the world, the people in small towns were always nicer than the ones in big cities. After Dhaka, the fresh air and friendliness felt medicinal.

When we reached the gates of the tea plantation, we were invited in. The man at the desk chatted with Dave, letting him know that we were free to ride around the tea gardens, but that a tour of the tea factory would not be possible that day. (We hadn't even known that was an option.) Dave asked about the three-hour biking loop we'd found in a guidebook, and the two of them discussed the details of it. I watched from the background as an invisible woman, the relieved introvert in me at odds with my outraged feminist.

The gardens themselves were incredibly peaceful. Row after row of dark green, chest-high tea bushes were dotted with working women. As they filled enormous shoulder bags with the light green top growth, the women called to each other, pointing, smiling, and waving as we passed. In the fresh air and relative solitude, it felt so good to be out of the city.

Eventually, we turned onto an old, red, beaten brick path, the beginning of our "three-hour loop." I laughed as we bounced down the bumpy trail— even singing like a Munchkin in the Wizard of Oz, "Follow the Yellow Brick Road *Follow the Bumpy Red Road*," just to hear my shaky voice. However, an hour later and still on the brick path, it was no longer amusing to me. My munchkin voice and boobs had grown tired of jiggling, as had my aching spine. Still, we vibrated along in that way for another couple of hours until, suddenly, Dave's bike chain went clattering to the ground behind him!

Great Oz! Now what? I thought, and we assessed the situation.

We were almost four hours into a circular three-hour ride, and that hadn't seemed to circulate. How much further could it possibly be? In the end, we decided to continue ahead, rather than turn back. We had never been alone before in Bangladesh, such a densely populated country, so surely we would meet someone soon. Besides, there was still plenty of daylight.

I stuck Dave's broken chain in the wire book carrier behind his seat, and for a while we see-sawed along. I'd build up speed from behind, riding up next to Dave, and giving him a solid shove forward, using my right arm to push on his back to give him momentum. He'd coast along for several more feet, sort of slithering his front wheel to stay upright as long as possible, until my next boost. However, after twenty minutes of that, we realized the chain had fallen out, and we'd lost it altogether. At that point, we just got off and walked our bikes.

Thirty minutes later, we finally reached the end of the brick path. There stood a group of young men talking, and we made our way over to see if anyone spoke English. Incredibly, just then, a work truck pulled up from behind us with a man shouting and waving Dave's bicycle chain in the air! He returned it to us with a smile.

One of the young men in the group spoke a bit of English, and we explained our situation. Cell phone calls were made and the group determined that we should follow one guy to his village. Dave and I blindly did so, putting our fate completely in his hands. He led us to a little village nearby, through a small collection of houses, and told us to wait in a central grassy area. Then, he took Dave's bike and disappeared.

"Do you think he'll come back?" I asked.

"I hope so," Dave laughed.

We had a good feeling about the guy.

As we waited, we sat down on the grass to rest, and a crowd of children gathered to look at us. They'd been racing old bike tires with sticks, running alongside the wheels to keep them upright. We showed interest in their game, in part to get the focus off of us. I thought it was encouraging to see bike parts, too.

Soon, along came a man in his 60s who introduced himself in strong English as Mr. Mabub. A village elder, he invited us back to his home. On the way we made the usual introductory chit-chat about where we were from and did we have children? Dave had a grown daughter, but we didn't have kids together so, naturally, Mr. Mabub asked if I had reproductive difficulties, as one does when first meeting a complete stranger.

"Why no children? You have problem?" he asked, pointing to my womb.

"Uhh, nope. No problems in here," I smiled tensely and patted my trusty uterus.

His head bobbled from pity to bafflement and back again.

When we got to his house, Mr. Mabub showed us into the front yard, instructing an older boy to find us a plastic table and chairs. The kids and several adults had followed us through the village and gathered at the edge of Mr. Mabub's yard, along a low fence to watch our visit.

"Welcome Brother and Sister," he said. "Please, sit, and have a drink."

A woman served us two hot Cloudy Lemon sodas and a packet of sweet crackers. These treats would have been a big expense for the family. We were honored, and I made a special effort to smile at and thank the woman.

We relaxed into our chairs. As we swallowed our first warm sip of soda, Mr. Mabub continued, "I just have one demand."

Dave sputtered and choked.

"Sir, you are from England," Mr. Mabub said to Dave, "Please, I need you to tell the British government that we would like to return to India."

Mr. Mabub went on to explain the situation to the best of his understanding. Later, I would do more research on my own.

Essentially, back in the 1850s during British rule of India, Indian workers were brought into what was then Eastern India to farm tea. Over time, those tea estates set up basic villages for the laborers, onto which new generations of workers were born. The region changed hands, first becoming East Pakistan and then Bangladesh, but the workers still identified as Indian. For a brief period of time during the Liberation War in Bangladesh in the 1970s, these Hindu laborers fled back to India to escape mass killings of non-Muslims in the area. However, there was nothing for them in India, so when it was safe, they returned to their homes on the tea estates after the war. The tea estates weren't much, deplorably inadequate really, but they offered homes, jobs, and even schools.

However, with the establishment of sovereign Bangladesh in 1971, the offspring of those tea workers continued to be born in Bangladesh without legal rights. Not Indian by birth, and not recognized by Bangladesh as Bangladeshis, several generations of these people were now what the United Nations referred to as "Internally Displaced Persons." They could not leave the plantations with rights to pursue free lives. And yet, without passports, they could not return to India. In the year 2011, they were still stuck on the plantations, essentially tea-slaves in a country that would not claim them.

At the time of our visit, Dave and I had no knowledge of Mr. Mabub's problem, and we knew very little about the larger situation. Later, when I approached a friend who worked in development for advice, I learned that there were hundreds of thousands internally displaced people in Bangladesh. Many were on tea estates, but the most critical situation was in the southeastern part of the country (in what would eventually become the world's largest refugee camp by 2020). The Rohingya people were living in far worse conditions, so the international community had focused its humanitarian aid there.

That day Dave stumbled out an inadequate reply, knowing that England would not take responsibility for tea plantation workers within Bangladesh. We suggested to Mr. Mabub, rather hopelessly, that he take their case to the Bangladeshi government, an action that had already been taken several times. We promised him we would look into it.

After our refreshments, Mr. Mabub dropped us off at another earthen home. There he introduced us to the village midwife, who spoke a little English, and her 19-year-old son, who seemed to be deaf. He and his mother communicated in what I suspected was homemade sign language. The young man was an artist and proudly showed us his collection of paintings hanging around the room. Also, something about his nature made me wonder if he was gay or perhaps nonbinary. It was none of my damn business, but if so, I worried for his safety, his very life, in that part of the world.

We settled in and admired the paintings. We also talked to the midwife about her profession. At one point, Dave mimed giving birth to a baby, and we all laughed heartily. I regaled the family with my ability to count to 10 in Bangla. Lovely people, they kindly hosted and entertained us while we waited for Dave's bicycle to be repaired.

Too soon, the young man who took Dave's bicycle returned. Cleaned, repaired, and oiled, the bike was in better condition than when we'd first got it. We thanked him generously, and tipped him in the same way. Mr. Mabub told us about a nearby bus stop, and how to catch it back to our hotel—our bikes could be put on the roof.

Holding hands with the people as they walked us to the edge of their village, we said our goodbyes. They were the world's forgotten people. Dave and I took a final look back, waved, and then biked out of their precious lives.

As the years pass, I sometimes think about those villagers, especially the midwife's son. He'd be in his early 30s now, perhaps with children of his own. That young person is a country-less, poor, brown, deaf, religiously-oppressed, possibly queer, tea-plantation slave. *And you think you got it tough?*

It's hard to know if my insufficient charity in South Asia made any lasting change in people's lives. I will always wish I'd done more. However, the kindness and compassion shown to me by the people of Bangladesh has made a huge difference in the big picture of mine.

GIGOLO SAFARI

Kenya, 2015

In 2015, Dave and I traveled to Mombasa, Kenya, from our home in Ethiopia for Spring Break. Four months after a pretty stressful winter holiday in Northern Ethiopia, we'd earned a more relaxing vacation. At the time, I hesitated to book a week on a beach because for years I'd been thinking and telling people "Oh, we're not really 'beach holiday' people." I'd soon learn that, actually, I'd been full of shit.

We booked a guesthouse, a kitesurfing resort, alongside the Indian Ocean. Dave and I figured we'd give kitesurfing a try, and do some scuba diving. The place was owned and run by a family of white Kenyans. Grace, the oldest daughter, managed the guesthouse. She was a kitesurfer, and an athletic, ambitious, young mother that I guessed to be about 30 years old. She checked us in, as her shirtless, tanned, white-blond toddler (a daughter) rifled through brochures on a coffee table. Grace said the guesthouse had been their family holiday home before she and her mother converted it to accommodate guests. In a matter of minutes, I grew a big crush on Grace. I wanted to be her when I grew up.

After we checked in, Dave and I settled into our room and headed to the porch café. I ordered an iced coffee and once again flipped through the guidebook. I had already noted that the area offered several interesting attractions: kitesurfing, scuba diving, a monkey trust, an old mosque, an elephant sanctuary, a shark trust, and safari trips inland. We could book those outings at our guesthouse or in one of several tourism shops in town; however, I felt a need to take it easy. We already lived in a developing country, so, to me at that time, sightseeing in Kenya sounded more exhausting than exciting. My laziness disgusted me, but it also outweighed me.

On the porch that morning the thing that most caught my eye in the guidebook was written in the warning section, "Be aware that there are many prostitutes and gigolos in local bars." I shot to attention!

Gigolos! Really?

I immediately began humming David Lee Roth's 1985 remake of *Just a Gigolo*. I'd memorized all the words the year it came out, back when I was nine years old. Had I stumbled onto a magical place in the world where the men are so skilled in the sack that women travel thousands of miles to pay for sex? Really? Was it a genetic gift or were there, like, technical schools? How fantastic! My mind was full of questions. How would a woman know when she'd encountered a gigolo? Would he wear gold chains against his hairy chest, or would the signs be subtler—long fingers and wiggly eyebrows? The jaded traveler in me suspected the whole thing was just a gimmick for tourists. *Special skills, my ass.* It was probably like getting a bad massage—just greasy and unsatisfying. Still, I was fascinated.

I ignored the librarians in my head, who shrieked like banshees when I dog-eared the page in my guidebook and smacked it shut. I got out my pen and notebook to start a plan. It would be my holiday mission to spot one of these elusive males.

Unfortunately, I wasn't quite sure where to begin. As a woman getting closer to 40 and, luckily, looking the part in her swimsuit, I felt I might be in the right demographic to, you know, lure one in. Mind you, of course, I had no intention of paying for the services of a gigolo. I had Dave for bedroom acrobatics. But I wanted to *see* a real gigolo. Maybe even buy him a drink and get a photo with him.

Let's take a moment to back up. *Of course,* I believe it is horrendous when people of any kind find themselves forced into prostitution, no matter where they might land on age, gender, or sexuality spectrums. Absolutely nothing about human oppression was or is humorous to me. Mind you, I have compassion for victims of human trafficking and personal circumstances, for victims of societal-shaming, and also for sex workers who don't consider themselves victims.

But, at the time—as a woman who had taken Sociology 101 in university—I was hardpressed to think of a single population in the world where *women* had browbeaten *men* into sex slavery. To my ignorant mind, a woman's gigolo probably wasn't a professional niche that would pay the bills. I figured at best it would be a side hustle, just a little extra meat to thunk on the dinner table. If, during my far-flung travels, I had somehow stumbled across an exotic land where progressive adult women paid entrepreneurial adult men for sex, I had some serious investigating to do.

"Sir, I'm gonna need some blue eyeshadow," I announced.

I wish I could say my vacation was filled with male prostitutes, but actually it was quite tame. Each day that week I painted on my secret weapon, a seductive shade of royal blue eye shadow. Dave pretended to be embarrassed, but I could tell he was even more attracted to me. I'm sure it's no surprise to learn that he was a terrible wingman on this quest. In large part, I blame Dave for my trouble attracting male sex workers.

Actually, other than my lewd eyeshadow, our vacation was almost wholesome. Our guesthouse was perfect, set on the longest, prettiest beach I think I've ever seen. The sand was pure white and so fine it was more like silt. About half a mile out, a sandbar broke the waves, creating a shallow calm beachfront, perfect for young children or for people learning to kitesurf. Wooden sailboats, hand-carved from tree trunks, dotted the horizon.

Later that first day, we put on our swimsuits and random, inadequate, swipes of sunscreen, before taking an all-day walk down the beach. So, for the rest of the week, we were shade-bound, taking early sunrise swims before the Equator's sun could flash-fry us again. During that week we ate lazy breakfasts under towering coconut trees as our waitress Lillian protected us from the monkeys with a slingshot. (*Talk about a fantastic job! I should ask Grace if she's hiring.*) We read books, lounged in hammocks, and drank beers at 10 a.m. just because we could. I gave Honey, the guesthouse's old Golden Retriever, little pieces of my breakfast bacon in exchange for fuzzy favors.

The lazy days blended together, our minds drifting with the waves.

"What do you think French people call French kissing?" I asked Dave, staring out into the water.

"Hmm? I don't know," he mumbled into his book.

"Just kissing, I suppose…"

In the afternoons, the wind picked up, and the kitesurfers came out. With harnesses around their torsos to help secure the massive, 20-ft (6-m) kites, riders hooked their feet into boards and surfed back and forth until sunset. I was surprised to see people of all ages, and I could tell it was a sport that would take a person several weeks to get good. A couple of lessons would only get me started. Due to our sunburns, however, Dave and I had to put off lessons until the end of the week, which was a mistake. The winds died, and ultimately, we missed our opportunity.

One day at dusk, as we waded down the beach back to our hotel through the rising tide, I looked over when I heard a *yelp!* Dave had disappeared, but his backpack was held suspended above the water by two shaky hands. He'd fallen into a tide pool, but managed to save the camera!

Another day, we went scuba diving, and I saw sea turtles the size of hubcaps! Unfortunately, I got seasick between our two dives, which chunkily overshadowed the swimming turtles. Somewhere deep underwater, while clearing my mask along with the puke from my sinuses, I lost my nose ring. For years to come, I liked to picture it resting on the bottom of the Indian Ocean, sea turtles gliding over a small sparkle from my old life in Bangladesh.

Dave also had a birthday that week. He turned 52. We celebrated with steak and coconut and rum milkshakes, in a beachfront restaurant under the stars.

All the while I kept my eyes peeled for gigolos and their Janes. There seemed to be aging foreign women conversing with young local men absolutely everywhere. A few times, I zoomed in with my camera and snapped photos for evidence, until it occurred to me later that this might be "in poor taste" so I deleted the pictures. *Boo.*

At other times, I scanned the bushes for middle-aged women to emerge disheveled and smug, until I gave the matter some deeper, faster, harder thought. Surely, any gigolo worth his salt would at least have a massage table. And some hand sanitizer.

"Where are all the people, anyway? Is it low season?" I asked a local beach peddler one day.

He was outfitted as a "Maasai warrior" in a burgundy cloth dress, a colorful beaded choker, and holding a small shield. It's possible he was truly Maasai, but he'd clearly dressed up for the tourists. As we spoke, he seductively fingered and stretched the enormous holes in his earlobes, showcasing them for me as we spoke. Still, I didn't think he was a gigolo.

"There is no 'season' now," he explained. "Kenya have very bad time."

Sadly, it was true. Between recent terrorist attacks at Garissa University in which 147 students were killed, and the fear of the Ebola virus (despite the nearest reported case being a 12-hour flight away), tourism in Kenya had plummeted in 2015. With so many people depending on tourism for their livelihood, the social effects of these horrific events had been devastating. The East African economy was hit hard.

To do our small part, Dave and I bought bracelets, key chains, sarongs, and massages, but there was no end to the selling. While I appreciated the entrepreneurship instead of just begging, we were soon stocked up and worn out. As two of only a few dozen tourists, Dave and I were targeted at every opportunity. It got to the point that when we saw a peddler coming, we'd start jogging down the beach. Our sheer athleticism, jiggling away in super-supportive swimsuits, was enough to deter most sellers. Self-preservation isn't always pretty.

"Here comes another one," I groaned, as a young man approached.

"Jambo!" he greeted.

We'd already exhausted ourselves from jogging, which had taken about 30 seconds. So, as we walked, we were forced to make panting chit-chat with the Rastafarian. Like many of the young men on the beach, he called me "Mama" since I was a mother figure. At 38 years old, his terminology burned me almost as much as the sun had done earlier in the week. Still, I'd signed up for it, years before, when I'd robbed the grave to get married. My husband *was* significantly older, so most people tacked a few extra years onto me. *Alas, hakuna matata.*

I suspected the beach peddler sold marijuana; however, Dave and I probably seemed too conservative a couple for him to make us that kind of offer. The Rasta played it safe, making small talk around the subject to suss us out. I imagine it was quite a surprise when I asked him where I could find a gigolo.

"A what?" he asked, confused.

"You know, a male hooker. I'm looking for a man prostitute."

I batted my baby blues. *Bink, bink, bink.*

The Rasta paused and took a step back to look at me.

"We do have this," he weighed in, "…but these men have sex with other men, not women."

Damn! I knew that type of professional exchange was the more likely scenario, but I was disappointed all the same. I'd really hoped this place would be different, a fantasy beach destination filled with talented, handsome young men and lonely, rich, horny, old women.

My face fell, and I went quiet. We changed the subject to our lives in Ethiopia and his in Kenya. We soon reached the end of the beach to part ways. We said our goodbyes, and Dave turned to go up the path, just a step ahead of me.

Suddenly, with Dave's back turned, the guy grabbed my hand, squeezed, and gave me an encouraging smile. He'd made a rash decision.

His eyes seemed to say, "Lady, I'd do it with you for free."

Then, he scanned my aging body a second time and steeled himself.

"Well, on second thought, since you are my first customer today, I will give you a good price—a very good price, indeed," his face renegotiated.

The young man caught me off guard. Uncomfortable and a little shocked, I shook my head "no," and pulled my hand awkwardly from his grip. I turned to follow my husband.

Then I caught myself. A voice inside me scolded, *That's enough, Amy. You jackass. To some people in the world this isn't a joke.*

I exhaled, turned, and called to the beach peddler as he strolled away.

"I'm sorry. Before you go, can I buy a couple of your bracelets, please?"

On our final night in Kenya, we went out to the beach, scattering crabs into the waves under the stars. Dave "paddled," lost in his own thoughts, as I sprinted back and forth. On that soft sand, my knees would let me, and for the first time in years I pushed my body hard, as fast as it could possibly go, back and forth under the moonlight. I took stock of my incredibly lucky life. Sure, I knew I'd worked very hard, and I'd made several good and tough choices along the way. Like most people, I'd experienced heartbreak and a few setbacks, too. And yet, *Amy, face it. You've had the luxury of wasting more opportunities than most people on this planet have ever even known. The world is a brutally unfair place, and you won the lottery. How will you make a difference?*

And later in bed, cocooned by mosquito netting within our little straw hut, I curled up against my husband. I felt so thankful for Dave, my family, and my health. It felt good to be alive, someplace between young and old, and on an adventure in Kenya with my best friend. I tried to suck the marrow out of the moment, not wanting that place and time to end.

I snuggled into my mate.

"Sir, can I have a kiss?" I asked.

"Sure..." Dave hesitated.

"But Madam, surely you realize—it's going to cost you."

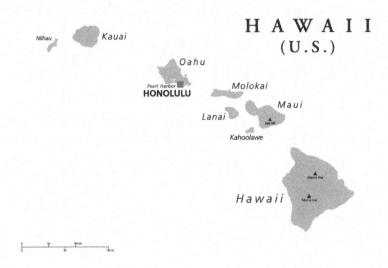

RUNAWAY

Hawaii, United States, 2017

"You should probably bring your cowboy boots, too," Mom suggested as she helped me pack. "You never know when you might need these."

I snatched my boots from her hands, huffed, and stuffed them into my already bulging, burgundy-and-pink-flowered suitcase. Along with a crumbling package of cheese crackers and three pairs of Days of the Week underwear, the bloated bag held a Swiss army knife, a Smurfs sleeping bag, a black Member's Only jacket, and my seven-year-old self's dirty little secret: "Kanky," my baby blanket.

"Of course, we'll miss you around here," my mom sighed, "...but I won't force you to stay. Since you aren't willing to clean the cats' litter box, it's probably for the best if you just go. I guess it's time for you to make your own way in the world."

I stiffened as she pulled me into a suspiciously dramatic goodbye hug. This wasn't how our battles usually went.

Of course, I knew she was bluffing, and she'd be sorry when I didn't come home. Plus, this time I had a plan. My teacher, Mrs. Stanley, had just read *My Side of the Mountain* to our class. Like that boy Sam who made a home in the woods, I could find a big tree to live in and survive on nuts and berries for weeks. "Jan" would beg me to come home before this was all over.

As I dragged my bulky suitcase out the front door, I looked back and glared at my mother. I wouldn't dare to say it aloud, but it thrilled me to think, *I'm so sick of this crap.*

Believe me, Sweetheart, her tired loving eyes mirrored, *the feeling is mutual.*

I was back by supper, just in time for my longsuffering mom to help me clean the cat box. She probably should have stuck to her guns, but she surrendered to love instead.

It's only fitting that I would end up married to a man who also saw the merit in a good run away.

Our connection started with dreams of exploring the world. When I first met Dave in 2002, I was a massage therapist and a part-time cocktail waitress in downtown Fort Worth, at a bar that served over 200 different sorts of beer. Dave was in the Royal Navy, but he was stationed in the USA. About twice a month, he'd fly from his home in Virginia to Texas to work on the Joint Strike Fighter project, collaborating with engineers and other pilots from around the world. Most of them stayed in the city center and flooded the restaurants and bars after work. So, despite the fact that Europeans were terrible tippers, I'd serve "Ackle" and his buddies something better than Glug Light.

In those days, I'd done very little international travel, but I had a chronic case of itchy feet. Meeting Dave, with his British accent, was like being introduced to an ambassador from the Big Wide World. As often as his work brought him to North Texas, Ackle grew to be a familiar face, a "regular" to banter with, and someone I always enjoyed. After my shifts ended, he and I spent countless hours in the pub over pints of Chimay Grand Reserve, Old Speckled Hen, and Paulaner Hefe-Weizen, discussing life and adventure.

Eventually, I changed jobs and moved overseas, but Dave and I stayed in loose touch. Each married to other people, our paths would cross, split, plunge, and plateau before winding up truly together. When Dave retired from the military at age 45, he visited me in Thailand and stayed. As a couple, nine years passed, working as teachers in Asia, Europe, and Africa, before we were able to achieve our goal and devote an entire year off to travel. Over 50 countries and 15 years after we first met in the pub, I saw that our story began like many of the greatest journeys in life—with good beer and big dreams.

Dave had been to Hawaii before, in the old days, prior to us being together. He had once made a whirlwind trip through the islands. On that visit he stayed in a fancy resort and packed so much into the 10-day vacation that he returned more tired than when he left. Of course, almost killing himself on the NaPali Coast Track may have played a role in his exhaustion.

The NaPali Coast Track, or Kalalau Trail, was a 22-mile, out-and-back hike on the northern edge of the oldest, northernmost island of Kauai. At that time, it was considered one of the most beautiful yet dangerous hikes in the world. Supreme athletes were able to complete the round trip in a single day, but most people took at least two, camping at the endpoint, on the gorgeous Kalalau Beach. The first time Dave came to Hawaii, he decided to take an uncharacteristically ill-prepared crack at the NaPali Coast Track, to see how far he could go in a single afternoon.

Of course, not actually being a supreme athlete, it didn't go well for Dave. However, he wasn't seriously hurt. Essentially, he pushed too far, underestimating the heat and amount of water needed. Dave ended up extremely dehydrated and desperately drinking from a waterfall on his way back. He's lucky he didn't get dysentery, or worse. Suffice it to say, the Kalalau kicked his ass, and then taunted him about it. So years later, when Dave returned to Kauai, he came prepared to conquer. I was there for backup.

"That's a lot of groceries for one person," I chuckled, striking up a conversation with a man in the campsite pavilion.

"Well, they're for the entire month," the man explained. "I live here full-time. That's my teepee around the corner." He continued to sort his provisions as his ride drove away.

Sometimes in life I came across people in the world who were *trying* to be eccentric. Other times I met folks who just were.

"Can you watch my stuff while I carry this over?"

At our nod, the man loaded his arms with economy-sized jugs of cooking oil and peanut butter and disappeared into the forest. His healthy, happy dog made trips back and forth with him.

It being a rainy evening, we spent most of dusk under the pavilion rather than out in our tent. So did 'The Mountain Man,' as we came to think of him. That night, as we cooked dinner and read books under cover, we continued to chat in bits to the fella. We learned that he was an oil painter who had been living in Hawaii since the mid-'80s. I'm fairly certain he'd read *My Side of the Mountain*, too, because it was clear he'd been living in the woods, successfully, for quite some time. We passed a pleasant evening in the shared space before heading to our tent to sleep. He wouldn't be the only mountain man encountered in Hawaii.

The next day, Dave and I made our way to the start of the Kalalau Trail. Rather than tempting thieves at the trailhead parking lot, we left our rental car at a campground and hitch-hiked the rest of the way. I'd only hitched twice in my life, and my mother would cringe to know my best fake smile snagged the first truck that came along. We piled into the back and perched on top of coconuts for the two-mile ride.

If supreme athletes were able to complete the Kalalau Trail in a single day, we figured that as two soft, drinky, middle-aged people, we ought to budget four. Besides, we didn't just want to survive the trek, we wanted to have hot tea with gingersnaps each evening. So, with loaded packs, we set out to camp three nights.

The trek itself was hard work—gorgeous, hard, sloppy work. Many people did the first two miles as a day-hike to a small beach, and because it had been raining, the beginning section was a muddy, slippery sludge pit. Our feet were caked heavy with mud as we climbed up and down river valleys, but the next day it dried out and opened into more level terrain with breathtaking views. It ended at Kalalau Beach where we found our personal 'Best Campsite Ever.' Jagged peaks, waterfalls, white sand, and blue sea—to find it, a person had to earn it, because boats weren't allowed to stop there.

"Sir, hold still a sec," I said to Dave. "I'm having a *mo*."

I stood on a rock and pulled him into a hug from behind. Over his shoulder, I took in the view.

The term *mo* was short for *moment*. Equal parts wonder and appreciation, it was how I described those unanticipated surges of gratitude that sometimes washed over me in life. Occasionally along the way, usually in nature, I was overcome with reverence. At those times, I stood still and tried to imprint the moment onto my heart, thinking, *I am so grateful for my life and this experience.*

That afternoon, on a little beach in the middle of the Pacific Ocean, we stood silently together and shared something sacred.

It was true that "Not all who wander are lost," but occasionally in life I came across someone who seemed painfully turned around.

On the track, we rounded a bend to see a man just off the path, picking and eating lychee fruit from a tree. Despite the heat, he was dressed in a heavy flannel shirt and jeans. As we approached I realized that his white skin was so pale that it had taken on a bluish shade. My instincts warred with my compassion, warning "Careful, Amy. This man is not well." He was definitely malnourished, and his mental health seemed questionable. Here was a person who had taken running away from home to another level.

I wondered if he had people in the world who worried about him, parents or a sister like mine, to cheer him on through good times and to help dust him off in bad. I hoped so, but doubted it. Not for the first or last time in my life, I felt deep appreciation for my loving family.

We passed this man twice, once on our way in and again on our way out. I left him with a smile and silently wished him wellness on his journey.

The last day, on the final stretch of the trail, we rejoined the day-hikers, those who made the two-hour day trip to that first little beach. Our egos were stroked as people commented on "what big packs we had," and I was reminded of one thing I love about my countrymen—their outspoken friendliness. We can be overwhelming but endearing, like Labrador Retreivers.

As we walked out, we met a chatty, animated young woman who was walking at our pace. She started a conversation with us. She opened with the usual, asking where we were from, always a complicated question for Dave and me.

"Oh, I'm from Texas and Dave is British," I countered, spoon-feeding her our details. "Where are you from?"

"I'm from Washington State. Seattle," she replied, dismissing her own story, "So do you guys live in the United States or England?

"Well, neither. We've been living in Ethiopia for the last three years. How about you? What do you do in Seattle?"

"Omigod! Ethiopia! What in the world were you doing over there! What was that like?"

So much for redirecting the conversation, she was off!

The trouble with having an international life was that it could be overshadowing in conversation. It often made us the center of attention, which made me a little uncomfortable. It was too easy to sound like an egotistical ass, and more often than not, it shut down my opportunity to learn about other people. When I met strangers for the first time, usually I tried to re-channel the chit-chat. However, in Hawaii, the young lady was tenacious in a nice way. She seemed genuinely interested, especially when we said that we were on a year off to travel. So I ended up telling her our story—that we had lived together in several different countries and that we were in the middle of our Midlife Gap Year.

Afterwards she said, "Gosh, your life sounds incredible. I can't imagine having been to all those places. My life has been so boring in comparison."

Her reply was part of the trouble with these conversations. People often couldn't relate, or they ended up feeling lame or defensive about their own lives. It could make connecting difficult. Dave and I didn't consider our path to be superior; it was just different, with peaks and pitfalls of its own.

I tried to explain.

"Thanks. I think my life has been amazing, but I realize that some people have no desire or no means to live abroad. And, honestly, it *is* a tradeoff. I miss being closer to family. My parents are getting older and my nephew is growing up, and that's tough. Also, I think it's getting harder for me to make and leave friends every couple of years. I'm getting worse at goodbyes. So, yes, absolutely, my life *is* incredible. I've had so many wonderful adventures. But, my heart is scattered all over the world."

She smiled and nodded as she considered my words. Overall, she seemed to like me and enjoy my story. However, there was always the possibility I'd sounded self-absorbed or overly sentimental—basically, like an ass. Whether she approved of me or not, I couldn't have said. I decided to leave that worry behind, on the NaPali Coast Track.

"Thanks for doing this with me," Dave said as we crossed the parking lot at the end of the trail.

"You bet," I shrugged, surprised at his gratitude.

As if I'd have it any other way.

I stopped and turned to really look at Dave, taking in crinkled blue eyes, a sunburned nose, and the satisfied grin peeking out from under his bucket hat. Covered in mud and sweat and funk—good Lord, the man was ripe. A hot mess.

Yep, I smiled from deep within. *I can run away all I want, but my home is where that one is.*

And amazingly, his tired loving eyes mirrored, *Believe me, Sweetheart. The feeling is mutual.*

DEATH OF A RIVER GUIDE

Tasmania, Australia, 2018

The following account is entirely true, *except for the parts that aren't.*
Also, the names and identifying characteristics of all characters have been
changed in order to protect the guilty. Enjoy the ride!

1

It was late in the season for a rafting trip. In Tasmania, autumn begins in
April, and the weather is turning. That year, in 2018, it was starting to get
chilly, and the realization that we were about to spend a cold, damp week in

wetsuits, rafts, and tents began to sink in. I wondered if Dave and I were more ignorant than intrepid, a not entirely uncommon theme in our adventures. At orientation the night before our big mission, I turned to raise my eyebrow at him. What the hell were we getting ourselves into?

Thanks to a monumental conservation effort back in the early 1980s, the Franklin River was (and is) still regarded as one of the world's last wild rivers. Thundering through the heart of an ancient temperate rainforest, the Franklin carved out one of Tasmania's deepest, narrowest gorges before opening into calmer waters surrounded by dramatic cliffs, odd rock formations, and caves that Aboriginal people had used almost 15,000 years ago. Its pristine caramel-colored waters, resulting from tannins in leaves, sustained quolls, wallabies, cockatoos, sea eagles, and the elusive platypus. The majestic Franklin was like no place else on Earth.

To adventure tourists, the river offered one of the most remote rafting adventures on the planet. Rapids ranging from Class I to Class VI required experienced guides who knew the river well enough to lead people through or around these perilous obstacles. With names like Nasty Notch, Sidewinder, Thunderrush, and The Cauldron, the Franklin was a dangerous place. There had even been a few deaths on the river. However, Dave and I had done the research, and we put our trust in the veteran rafting company we'd selected.

On the night of orientation, we met our group leader, Greg, a tall, lanky, river man in his early 40s, with a long, fading purple ponytail. Greg had a German accent, but I'd later learn his mother was Australian. An otter in an opera house, I suspected Greg was more expert in the river than he was up in front of groups. The special education teacher in me could see the hyperactive, sporty, distractible boy in him, so I tried to cut Greg some slack and hold tight to his flailing presentation. He explained the plan.

Because heavy rains had passed through Tasmania that week, with a possibility for more in the forecast, our seven-day rafting trip had been pushed back and cut short. The Franklin was dangerously high, and we had already postponed our leaving by one day. Also, because it was the company's last trip of the season, extending the trip to make up our missing days wasn't possible. "No worries," Greg said. We would cover the same distance by paddling longer days at a safer level.

I looked around the room at the other guests, 15 in total, including some teens. No obvious Olympians. The normal itinerary called for "average fitness," a term I'd found to be deceptively different, depending on the country using it. I wondered if it was the German or the Australian in Greg that thought our hodgepodge group could handle it. Regardless, how hard could it be?

Greg passed out large, watertight, storage barrels. About thigh-height and the circumference of a dinner plate, our personal items for the week would need to fit inside. After we got fitted for wetsuits, Greg arranged to pick us up from our hotels the next morning.

Early the following grey morning, the bus picked us up outside our hostel. We tossed our barrels into a towed trailer, and loaded onto the partially-filled bus. After winding through Hobart to pick up the others, we started the three-hour drive west to the put-in.

On the bus we began to meet our trip mates, an interesting cross-section of Australians. Other than the guides, two Germans and another Brit like Dave, we were the only foreigners. Observing our group was a fascinating window into Australian society for me, my own little sociological study (mindful that almost everyone was white, able-bodied, and able to afford a flipping expensive rafting trip). Aged 13 to 58, they came from across the continent.

We made it to the put-in about 11 a.m., but the river was still much too high. Greg decided we should wait, so the kitchen area, the lunch table, and the toilet were set up instead. The lunch spread was amazing, in part since seven days' food allowance was being spread over fewer days.

As with all backcountry adventures, 'What goes in must come out,' and using the bathroom was tricky. Number One was pretty straightforward, but deuces were especially scarring. All the while praying that someone wouldn't come bouncing down the wooded path just in time to witness the big event, a person started the process in the squat position. Next, one had to hold a rather small bag very close to where she imagined her butthole to be, then squeeze, and hope... Be it good aim or a sloppy recovery, the full baggie was double-bagged and tied off. This was finally squished into an increasingly unfortunate, community dry sack, which would raft with us for the duration of the week.

With no cell signal in the area, we interacted like cave people. The group shared backgrounds and told stories. We explored the area and hiked together. We spent hours sitting on grounded rafts around a makeshift, spinal backboard table, snacking and chatting as we killed time. However, as that first drizzly gray day wore on, Greg eventually made the call.

"Set up your tents. We won't be leaving today," he said.

"Oh and mind the leeches," he added. "Astrid found one on her leg the last time we did this trip."

I shuddered remembering my one experience with a leech, in the stone shower area of a rustic Himalayan hut. Waving like sea grass, it had stretched the length of my hand—long, thin, otherworldly. It reached out to cling to and prey on any unlucky passer-by.

"Leeches. Super!" I said to Dave.

We headed apprehensively into the woods to find a spot safe from blood-sucking.

Our seven-day trip was now down to five, and when we didn't leave again the following day—four.

Over those two days that we waited for the river to go down, personalities began to show themselves. There were 15 guests in total, including, *God help us*, three 13-year-olds. We came to know our four guides a bit better too. There was lanky Greg, whom we met at orientation, as well as two guides in their twenties: a charming Englishman with a pierced nose named Charles, and an Aboriginal/white Tasmanian called Clark who was built like a brick house. Clark's deadpan humor kept me guessing, but several women in our group, young and old, seemed to find him hilarious.

There was also Astrid, another German, who was Greg's partner in romance and business. A wiry white woman with dreadlocks and a sharp face and tone, Astrid was fierce. Astrid may have been a joint owner in the rafting company, but it was clear that she was also the boss, based on the way she snapped orders to Greg and the other guides. I was all for strong female leaders, but I was surprised by the way she spoke to those around her, especially the guests. *She's German*, I told myself after Astrid growled at me for walking through the kitchen area on my way to the bathroom. *She probably doesn't realize how rude she sounds.* I'd lived in Bavaria for a year, and to me it seemed that, stereotypically, Germans didn't waste time on pleasantries. It was an efficiency I actually appreciated, but the flip side was that Germans could sometimes seem abrupt and slightly scary, which were characteristics that hit pretty close to home. *Of course,* not all Germans are jackasses, but I was trying to give Astrid the benefit of the doubt.

Of all the families we met on that adventure, I was most drawn to a man named Peter and his three daughters. Like us, they'd lived internationally, and Peter had worked in developing countries, too. The two older daughters, Kate and Liz, were confident, well-spoken young women. However, at 17, the youngest daughter, Taylor, was just beginning to find her voice.

Naturally quiet and very soft-spoken, Taylor often let her older sisters and father do the talking. The youngest sibling like me, she tended to go with her family's flow. Also, unlike her older sisters, Taylor was adopted from Ethiopia. Having just finished a three-year posting in her birth country, I felt an immediate connection to the girl. In the midst of our big group of outspoken, colorful strangers, Taylor blended timidly into the background, taking it all in.

It was her older sister Liz who made an announcement that first night at dinner,

"Taylor has to write a science fiction story for English class at school. Does anyone have any good ideas?"

Our group took a few moments to toss out ideas and chew on them.

"…How about aliens?"

"Oh, you should do something with time travel…."

"…What about robots? Snake robots!"

The conversation soon moved on, but I thought about Taylor's assignment for a very, very long time.

Later that night, Jim, a twinkle-eyed Tasmanian, had us go around the circle to share our "talents." An awkward redheaded 13-year-old named Andrew made up two different raps about architecture. Quite an unusual mash-up, I thought, but we all just rolled with it. Pete, the father of the girls, recited a Shakespearean poem. Something came over me that night. I surprised myself by delivering the entirety of Madonna's *Vogue* chant, *Greta Garbo, and Monroe—Dietrich and DiMaggio…*" while my husband stared at me in open-mouthed disbelief. *Who is this woman?*

2

Finally, on what should have been the fourth scheduled morning of our trip, we hit the water. This meant that six days worth of paddling would be condensed into three. Little did we know that typical five-hour river days would grow to be ten hours. So much for "average fitness."

Charles woke us up at 5 a.m., shining a light outside our tent.

"Rise and shine! Time for breakfast."

We ate a quick meal, packed up our tents, and squeezed into our wetsuits, lifejackets, and helmets.

As the others arrived, we were separated into groups. After two days of speculation, we finally learned our raft teams. Dave and I would be in Astrid's boat with a single woman in her late 30s named Megan, who was a doctor. This meant our boat was a person down with only four people, but since Megan had medical skills, it seemed like a good tradeoff. Also, as a teacher on holiday, I was glad we didn't have any of the 13-year-olds in our boat. I loved kids, but we'd earned a break. Overall, I was worried that we were in Astrid's boat, given her gruffness, but I told myself to relax. I resolved to let it go, like water off a platypus' back.

As we set off that morning into the Collingwood River, about an hour from its confluence with the Franklin, Astrid organized our team of four. With some prior experience of boating, Dave and I had developed a little more paddle stroke efficiency than had Megan, a complete novice. Dave, a lefty, sat on the back left of the raft. Megan, still a bit of a lily-dipper when it came to paddling, sat parallel to him on the back right. Astrid steered the raft from the back center. I balanced us out on the front right. This put me in the most exciting seat, alone up in the prime splash zone. However, it being cloudy autumn, deep down in the shadows of the river canyon, I soon learned that getting wet was too cold to be much fun. Little did I know that there would be no real chance to dry out over the next several days.

A fully-catered experience, the raft was filled with our share of barrels, eight to ten in total, which sat behind Dave and Megan and in front of Astrid. Astrid talked us through the basic strokes and the importance of holding the paddle properly by its "T-grip" so we wouldn't blacken eyes or knock out teeth. She went through her commands: All Forward, Forward Right and Forward Left, Back Right and Back Left, (All) Back Paddle, Hang on! Get Down!

Astrid explained that the last order, "Get Down," would be crucial. This was reserved for the most dangerous rapids, when we were meant to duck down into the center of the boat, grab the rope, and hang on for dear life. We practiced a few strokes as we got started. By the time the Collingwood joined up with the tawny waters of the Franklin River, we felt as ready as we'd ever be.

That first day on the river was wild. At its maximum runnable level for commercial rafters, the current was pushy and the guides had to be on their games. It was clear early on that Astrid was feeling some stress.

We struggled to keep up with Astrid's commands as she adjusted and then readjusted our position in the water. In the space of 30 seconds she'd bark, "All Forward! Forward left. Back right. Back Left! BACK LEFT!" To make matters worse, I could hardly hear her up front, over the roar of the water. It was difficult to follow her blurring commands so our crew had trouble finding its rhythm.

It's no surprise that we ran into trouble early. Midmorning, as we approached one of the first tricky spots, a series of rock obstacles and ledges, our raft was "Sweeper," the last in the group. We watched as the first three boats negotiated their way down in turns. It looked fun, exciting, and technical. My heart was pounding.

On our turn, with confusing ferocity, Astrid shrieked commands as we advanced through the raging water. Things got off to a smooth start, but soon went pear-shaped. Despite our best effort, the boat got hung up on a rock just above a cascading ledge. From there we bounced ourselves free— pop, pop, popping up and down until the raft worked itself free. At the river's mercy, we slid off the rock and over the ledge only to get caught again on another rock just below. The raft began to fill with water from the cascading overflow above. In seconds, the raft filled and flipped upside down, dumping us all into the frigid current.

I'd been swimming as long as I'd been walking in life so, thankfully, I wasn't easily traumatized in water. That day, spilling into the freezing river exhilarated and amused me at first. I maintained the whitewater swimmer's position, on my back with my nose and toes out of the water. I floated downstream a bit until I could scramble onto a rock, just off the edge of shore.

Unfortunately, I got stranded there, unable to jump to land without risk of being swept further downstream.

I looked back to see that Megan, Dave, and Astrid were upstream from me on the shore. Our raft was upside down, lodged between a rock and the river's edge. Fortunately, our barrels had remained strapped down into the raft, but they made the raft extremely heavy. My shipmates were having one hell of a time trying to turn the raft back over.

A charmer to the core, Astrid screamed me over to help. When she realized that I wasn't able to get off my boulder in the river, she came over to give me a hand. Extending the paddle to me, I was able to grab hold and launch myself onto the shore, with Astrid pulling me in as I jumped.

Once I made it to shore, the four of us tried to leverage the raft back over. However, even with our combined weight, it wouldn't budge. Eventually, Clark—the most athletic, strongest of our guides—left his raft and swam back upstream to help right our boat.

Shaken and quiet with chagrin, we reloaded. I suspected that Astrid's ego had taken a bit of a hit for misdirecting her guests into an icy swim, as well as for her struggle to turn over the raft without help from one of the other (male) guides. Teeth chattering and bodies shivering, our crew somberly paddled to rejoin the others.

"Amy, hold on a minute," said Dave a bit later. "Don't panic. Just be still."

"What is it? What's on me?" I freaked, his false calm triggering my irrational fear of bees and other small, fast things.

"I think there might be a leech on your neck," Dave replied evenly. "Come here."

"Get it off! Get it off!" I panicked, stumbling back over the center raft bumper toward him. In the process, I accidentally let go of the T-grip of my paddle, and almost blackened Dave's eye.

"Watch your paddle!" Astrid barked from the backseat.

"Hold still," he commanded in a whisper, and he rubbed firmly across the back of my neck.

There was no pain, only a strange tugging pressure.

"Yep, it's a leech. It looks like a baby," Dave said.

In his hand, I saw a small bloody black slug-like creature. Dave cut it in half with his thumbnail and flung its guts back into the water.

"Yuck. Do you see any more on me?" I whispered, shuddering. I was a little embarrassed by my outburst since I was in the company of two tough women.

Dave gave me a quick scan, and thankfully found nothing else.

"Here, let me check you," I said.

"Would you guys mind checking me?" asked Megan.

The three of us were clear.

Half an hour later, at a calm spot, I tried to be constructive. "Astrid, we were trying to follow you, honestly. But it's really hard to hear you over the water." To this, she rolled her eyes.

Dave and I looked at each other. *Wow. Did that really just happen?*

At the next slightly technical place in the river, Astrid shouted, "Forward right. Forward Right! FORWARD RIGHT! CAN YOU HEAR ME NOW?" Mocking and totally unnecessary because the water feature wasn't large or loud, her tone was foul. It was just plain bitchy.

Megan, Dave, and I were all were shocked into silence, flabbergasted that she would speak to anyone, especially paying patrons, like that.

On very few occasions in life had I been boggled to meet a person like Astrid, one who had survived to adulthood, and even thrived in it, behaving like a total ass. A bully. On this occasion, I wondered:

1. How can a person make it into her 40s and still behave like this?

2. Has she not seen all the Internet memes on empathy?

3. Was there no sister (like mine) in Astrid's childhood to bite the ever-loving tar out of her when she behaved horribly?

4. Am I the person to rectify Astrid's poor behavior?

"Why don't I just repeat the commands after Astrid?" Dave jumped in, since he knew how my gears clicked.

"Thanks. That'd be nice," Megan agreed. "I've been having trouble hearing, too."

3

We ran all kinds of rapids on that first day. Most were fun, but some tipped the balance toward scary. More than once we were commanded to "Hang on!" and alone up front, I lost my grip on the rope and was slammed into the bottom of the boat. It helped that Dave was repeating the commands, and I resolved to have my hearing checked soon. Thankfully, we didn't swim again.

There were also several sections we bypassed on land because they were too dangerous to ride through. Tethering the rafts with ropes, the guides had us scramble up and around on land as they safely lowered the boats down-stream. Empty of people, yet full of our gear, we watched the ruthless current batter our transport and livelihood.

"Wow! Look at that!" I said to Dave, perched on a cliff side as we watched one raft descend through a thundering pool.

"Can you imagine being in that boat right now?" I asked him.

"Hell, no. A person would be lucky to survive," Dave replied.

As ever, the power and beauty of nature astounded us. On this trip, however, we flirted with disaster by staring into its eyes.

I wish I could say that Astrid grew to be nicer, but she actually seemed to get worse. Megan and Dave had more patience with her. Dave, a former fighter pilot, and Megan, an emergency room doctor, were used to dealing with people who were under huge amounts of stress. Dave had been through pilot training, where cadets were pushed to find their actual breaking points, adding pressure and difficulty until the trainee was so strained that they were unable to successfully perform their duties. Dave understood that Astrid was approaching her maximum stress level, so he had an easier time, if not excusing her, understanding her. Plus, he'd lived with me for a decade.

Personally, I was ready to smack her in the face with my paddle. I wasn't alone in feeling frustration. As the trip continued with Astrid barking orders throughout the rapids, portages, and even during mealtimes, the other guides and guests began to bristle at her tone.

"What is wrong with you?" Astrid shouted at 13-year-old redheaded Andrew for taking off his helmet during one portage. I doubt she realized what I knew through conversation with his father, that Andrew had mild autism, formerly known as Asperger's.

"Excuse me?" his father countered. "Watch how you speak to my son," Aaron grumbled under his breath, just loud enough to be heard. Astrid seemed unfazed.

Mind you, Andrew taking off his helmet was incredibly foolish, and Aaron should have been more actively parenting. But still. Astrid was way out of bounds.

Seething inside, I glared at Astrid, but I found myself drawn up short with concern. The pallor of her skin shook me. Also, Astrid's red eyes had dark purple circles underneath, and her thin frame seemed swollen to me. We were all freezing, especially the five of us who had swum (including

Clark), but being a small woman who was likely more prone to hypothermia, Astrid really did not look well.

I granted another pardon. *Amy, give her a break. She's struggling, too.*

As the day progressed, we found a routine, alternating between runnable rapids and portages. There were dozens of both. It was strange to develop comfort so near potential disaster, but we got used to the mighty waters of the Franklin. Despite the cold and my initial anxiety, my "fight or flight" response settled into "monitor and manage." I was even able to have some fun.

Nonetheless, later in the day there was a truly wild moment. The group planned to climb around yet another killer rapid, but we would then need to paddle through an intense second rapid just below the first. There was a small eddy in between, where everyone would reload before attacking the next river feature.

All was going to plan, and we had rope-lowered three boats successfully. Those passengers were reloaded and waiting in the eddy. Meanwhile, Dave, Megan, and I stayed on the rocks since our raft was last and still getting lowered. Greg and Astrid managed the ropes upstream. Ross and Clark waited with the guests, supporting the production from downstream.

However, the river current was strong, and with three rafts already inside the small eddy, the fit was tight and precarious. It was difficult to hold onto the ropes. In horror, I watched as the boat, with two fathers and two young teen sons, was swept from the eddy into the current *without their guide*!

Their raft plunged into the boiling rapid below. With dads in the front and boys in the back, the raft bounced and spun perilously through the whirlpool. They paddled furiously, and with dumb luck, managed to make their way into an eddy beneath the turmoil.

At the bottom the boys were stoked, cheering and high-fiving with ignorant bliss! Chests swelled with adrenaline and pride, it was clear the boys felt like men. Equally, I'm sure their fathers aged ten years in those few seconds. *When we get home, let's not tell your mother about this.*

After an arduous, overcast, 10-hour paddling day, our group split to make camp for the night. One half camped together on a small shore on river left. Thankfully, our raft was paired with Peter and his daughters on river right, so we were able to enjoy a quieter evening after an exhausting day.

Dave and I unpacked our barrels and set up our tent. Then we peeled off our clammy wetsuits to discover all sorts of river goodies in the dank folds of our bodies—leaves, silt, fungi. Mercifully, neither of us had leeches. I dusted off and bundled up into my fleece pajamas, puffy jacket, and woolly hat, warm for the first time all day.

We sought out hot drinks in the kitchen area, where we found the guides setting up for the evening meal. With typical tact, Astrid directed Clark:

"Did I say to stack those plates?"

"Come here and take this. No, not that. THIS!"

"No, not over there. Damn it! Just. Put. It. Down!"

Judging by his face, it was clear that Clark was seething. Like many of us, he'd had enough of Astrid's mouth.

There was no fire, but folks had started to gather around some snacks resting on a backboard and barrel table. I found a spot on a log next to Taylor, the quiet 17-year-old. We sipped on hot chocolate as we waited for dinner, which, to Astrid and Clark's credit, ended up being fantastic. I'd learned to never underestimate the difference a warm meal can make in the backcountry. However, the catering on this trip was top notch—truly outstanding.

By this time in life I'd also learned that the best party conversations happen in the corner with the quiet people. Sitting with Taylor was no different. A smart, sensitive, straightforward young woman, Taylor told me about school, life in Perth, and her favorite musician. In turn, I told her our story, that we were teachers taking a year off work, and we were currently on the last leg of our trip—two months in Australia.

As we talked, I unpeeled a banana from the bottom up because I'd read a hack online that doing so left fewer strings on the fruit. (It worked!) We shared a deep laugh when Taylor asked if all Americans peeled bananas like that—just more evidence to support our childhood notions that our two countries were upside-down opposites. We also had a great conversation about Taylor's plans for her science fiction story, which led into a deeper conversation about the transformative power of writing.

"Do you really think writing about something hurtful can make a person feel better about it?" Taylor asked.

"Honestly, Taylor, I'm not sure. What do you think?"

We two writers chewed it over, and both promised to give it a try.

After dinner, Taylor and I volunteered to wash up, so we headed down to the water's edge to bring up some buckets. By this time it was dark outside, and we carefully picked our way to the shoreline, trying not to turn an ankle on the steep slope or dark rocks.

When we got to the water, I found a large flat rock from which I was able to fill my pail. Taylor, however, struggled to find a level area.

Splash! "Yeep!"

I looked over to see that Taylor had lost her footing, and had fallen in up to her knees.

"Oh no, Taylor! Are you okay?"

I quickly reached out and pulled her to firmer ground, but her sandals, socks, and sweatpants were soaked. A trooper, she brushed off my concerns, and we made our way back up to the others. Poor girl. I was certain she would have a cold miserable night in her tent.

4

The next morning, I dreaded three activities in equal measure—putting on my frigid damp wetsuit, shitting into a baggie, and getting back into that boat with Astrid.

I wasn't the only one off to a rough start. At breakfast, Taylor looked awful. Her bloodshot eyes made it clear she hadn't slept well, and she was uncharacteristically grouchy. She growled at her father before storming off, "Why did we have to come on this stupid trip anyway?"

Unlike Taylor, the current that morning was tranquil. The roaring Franklin had softened into russet ripples against moss-covered stones, and I finally remembered to breathe.

I took a moment as we paddled along to give myself a talking-to: *Amy, you can't let Astrid's behavior ruin your day. Look at this beauty around you. This is a once-in-a-lifetime experience. You're healthy, with the person you love, and living what might be the most amazing year of your life. Remember, let this go, like water off a platypus's back.*

I swear to Oz, a few minutes later, just under the tawny surface of the river, I saw one! A platypus splashed up to the surface for a quick second, before diving deep and swimming away. I was the only person on our raft to spot it.

Later, when I told Taylor's dad Peter that I'd seen a platypus, he smiled deeply.

"Amy, I hope you realize how lucky you are. Even most Australians have never seen a platypus in the wild! So treasure it."

Later that morning, the current soon picked up, and there was still plenty of action the second day. Our group soon found its familiar routine, either attacking or circumventing rapids. On this day, the guests were increasingly involved in helping to portage the rafts down the river, anchoring our boats with ropes to trees and rocks. Sometimes we stacked one raft on top of the other as we lowered them down.

At every opportunity Dave volunteered to help, mostly because that's who he is, but also because the others in the group, aside from Andrew's dad Aaron, didn't step up to help. We needed two or three people to hold the rope in an anchored line. They worked together to frenziedly pull the raft to shore.

Dave helping made me a little uneasy because it wasn't fail-safe. Plus, while this didn't make a huge difference, at 55 he was the second oldest man on the trip. At any moment, his hands could have been seriously burned, he could have been pinned against a rock, or he might have been pulled into the raging waters. At times I tried to pitch in to help, but so near the furious current I was feeling flustered. I knew me being timid was dangerous, so I backed off and left it to those who had more confidence.

Two guests, Jim and John, our Tasmanian comic relief, started refer-ring to Dave as "Special Ops" because they knew he'd been through survival training in the military and because he was so keen to help. Jim winked at me as he teased Dave, offering advice from the sidelines.

I bantered back, "Laugh it up, Jim, but this makes me nervous. I'm the only one here that will worry for more than half an hour if Dave gets swept downstream. The rest of you will just move on to what's for lunch." As with many of my jokes, it was a smidge too blunt to be funny, and Jim's face fell. But, at the next portage, he stepped up to help my husband.

There was a dramatic and dangerously close call that afternoon, again while avoiding a rapid too dangerous to take on.

This incident, not unlike the father-son heart stopper, started in a simi-lar fashion. Three of four empty rafts had been lowered through a death trap. The guides were working together to drop the last one.

Meanwhile, like many adventure sport tourists, several guests had grown obliviously blasé in the face of danger, and so sat chatting on the rocks as the guides toiled. After all, the trip had cost an immense amount of money.

Hell, for the price we'd paid, we all should have ridden down in the pockets of mother-luvin' marsupials.

However, Dave, Megan, and I remained on guard, probably because Astrid had kept us on high alert for two days. The others hadn't swum the first day, so they weren't fighting low-level hypothermia. Plus, their guides were always, at minimum, pleasant. I suspected my trip-mates were having a very different, more relaxed, even fun experience. Imagine! However, in this instance, our vigilance served us well.

As the last raft went sailing past, the rope slipped loose from its anchor point, a riverside rock. This left Greg holding the rope alone. To save himself, he wisely let go. The final unmanned raft and all its gear went roaring downstream.

"Go! Go! Go!" Astrid shouted, to which no one responded because Astrid always yelled.

"In the rafts! Get in the rafts!" Greg echoed.

I was one of the first to recognize what was actually happening.

"Everyone up! Get into the boats. It doesn't matter which one. We have to catch that raft!" I shouted.

I stirred and directed the large group efficiently into action. Who says it doesn't pay to be a schoolteacher?

Guides Clark and Charles were quick to react, as well as a mish-mashed boatload of others. They quickly pushed off to chase down the runaway raft. The rest of us loaded up, willy-nilly into random rafts, and followed close behind.

Not for the first or last time that trip did Clark's athleticism saved the day. As the second raft neared the runaway first, he launched himself into the empty boat and was able to single-handedly steer it into an eddy.

We regrouped on the shore, forcefully laughing with relief.

Taylor was not amused.

"What's wrong with you people?" She shouted at the group. "You think this is funny!"

Everyone stopped and stared.

"Easy, Taylor," her sister Kate soothed. "It's okay. We're all okay."

"Kiss my ass, Kate!" Taylor hissed. "You aren't my mother. Don't treat me like a child."

"Taylor Alison Campbell," Peter warned. "No, she isn't your mother, but I'm your father. You need to apologize to your sister and these people."

To this Taylor flipped double birds and stomped over to sit in her grounded raft. There, she stared out into the river, mindlessly scratching her shins.

Astrid laughed inappropriately, but the rest of us sat in stunned silence.

"I'm so sorry about this," Peter apologized to the crowd. "She isn't herself," he explained, and made his way over to his youngest daughter.

I'd seen teenagers at their worst, but Taylor's behavior truly surprised me. I didn't know her well, but this wasn't the person I'd shared a banana with the night before. Something serious was going on.

Astrid's behavior no longer surprised me. I wish I could say I'd heeded my own advice to let it go, but I'd grown livid instead. It was one thing to mistreat me, but I couldn't stand the way Astrid spoke to my husband.

As we got going again and pulled away from shore, Andrew lost hold of his paddle. Luckily, Dave managed to fish it out, just as the current grabbed both rafts.

"Give it to him! They need that paddle!" Astrid barked in urgency.

Dave was unsure of quite what to do since the other raft was about 10 feet (3 m) away in rushing waters.

"Come on! Do it!" Astrid screeched.

Startled into action, Dave tossed the paddle toward the other raft, clearly worried about hitting someone in the head. Admittedly, it wasn't a great throw, but it got there. Barely.

"Are you serious? What was that?" Astrid scolded.

"You asked me to give them the paddle. I'm doing the best I can, Astrid!" Dave growled back, defending himself.

"Not like that, *Vollidiot*. That was terrible!" Astrid berated.

Whatever she'd said in German, I could tell it wasn't nice, and my charitable husband had long since lost his patience with this woman. I watched him choke back his anger, and I seethed in my own. And to think we'd paid an enormous amount of money to be treated this way. I was gobsmacked.

Sometimes truth is stranger than fiction.

5

At our lunch stop that day, the sun briefly came out for the first time in over three days. Clark used the opportunity to strip his wetsuit off, down to the waist. Several of the young and older single ladies used that opportunity to appreciate the view. Not an ounce of fat on his 29-year-old body, Clark's appeal seemed to reach most demographics.

I used this opportunity to check in with Taylor. I'd never been good at comforting people. I usually left that to the more natural nurturers. But I felt like Taylor and I had a budding friendship and mutual respect for each other. Plus, I was genuinely worried about her.

She sat on the shore away from the others, scratching her legs and throwing rocks into the water. As I got closer, I was shaken by her appearance. She looked terrible!

Her bloodshot eyes had only gotten redder with dark circles underneath. It was clear that she had been crying, but it shocked me to see pink tear stains down her cheeks. Was that blood? Plus, her fingers were bleeding and a couple of nails were torn and broken. I guessed from all the scratching. What was going on here?

"Hey, Taylor," I said gently as I approached. "Are you okay?"

Taylor startled, not having heard me approach.

"Leave. Me. Alone," she gritted out.

I paused and then sat quietly nearby. Together we silently watched the current for a few minutes.

As we sat, Taylor began to furiously scratch her legs, and inadvertently gasped when she gouged an especially tender spot.

"Let me see," I lulled.

"No, it hurts too much," she whispered, her voice broke with emotion.

"Come on. Let me see," I tried again.

Taylor nodded her head and began to roll up the leg of her wetsuit. As she did so, a stream of blood trickled down her leg.

"Oh God, Taylor! We have to clean that up. I'm going to get the medicine kit. I'll be back."

I raced over to collect her family. Peter was deep in conversation on the other side of the beach, but I was able to grab Kate from the lunch table and to pull Liz away from

The Clark Show. We snatched the medicine kit and rushed back over to Taylor.

Between the three of us, we were able to coax Taylor into a sheltered area behind some bushes. There we slowly and gently helped her to remove the wetsuit, folding it down over her bathing suit. It was still basically dry so that made things easier. When we got to her knees, Taylor cried out.

"I know it hurts, Taylor, but we have to do this," I persisted. "I think it will feel better to do it quickly, in one big pull."

"Okay," Taylor agreed. And after a few deep breaths, she said, "I'm ready."

We removed Taylor's shoes and had her sit on a rock. With the wetsuit bundled just above both knees, we counted to three. "One, Two, Three!"

We yanked, jerking the wetsuit inside out over both feet.

Taylor screamed out.

Kate, Liz, and I gasped in.

Both of Taylor's legs below the knee were covered in thick shiny black leeches, the size of my middle finger. It was clear that she had been scratching, too, because the tails and bodies of some had squirted and smeared across her skin, leaving bloody black skids. Long deep fingernail marks scored both legs.

"We have to get these off of you!" Kate directed.

Liz, not the least bit squeamish, grabbed hold of one and pulled it from Taylor's leg.

It made a tiny squeal as it released, and Liz swiftly smashed it on the ground with a rock. Blood and yellow-green guts spurted out.

Taylor was silently crying by this point. Bloody tears streamed down her face as we pulled the leeches from her legs and smashed them.

"Eeeek!" Splat. "Eeeek!" Splat. "Eeeek!" Splat.

There were 11 all together. Judiciously, Kate found and killed two more that were hiding inside Taylor's crumpled wetsuit.

After we finished checking her legs, Taylor asked me for some privacy and her sisters helped to check the rest of her body. She was clear. So, we cleaned her wounds and her teary face, and then we all headed over to tuck into some ham sandwiches and lamington cake.

We reached our camping spot at twilight, another 10-hour day behind us. My shoulders were killing me.

This time, instead of setting up our tents, we would be sleeping under rock ledges at the base of a massive rock wall. Aboriginal people, from the oldest human culture in the world, had been sheltering in crevices like these for almost 40,000 years.

That night, dinner was uncharacteristically quiet. We were all exhausted and famished. Scattered on the rocks near the delicious food, we ransacked the snack table and scarfed down hot quesadillas as quickly as the guides could take them off the burner.

Taylor had recovered and was back to her sweet self. She took a moment and made an announcement to the group.

"I'm sorry for the way I acted earlier, everyone."

"No drama, sweetheart," reassured Grace, the only mother on our trip. "I think we've all felt some stress on this trip. Gabby and I got into a bit of a biffo this morning in our tent," She laughed. "Come over here and sit by us, darling."

That all settled and behind us, the group chatted quietly between mouthfuls.

"Man, these shrimp quesadillas are good!" I mentioned to Dave.

"Yours have shrimp? Mine have been plain cheese."

"Well it's some kind of meat. I guess it could be chicken."

As I wolfed down my next bite, I began to choke on some stringy cheese that I'd only managed to half swallow. With the top end still in my mouth and the other end inside my throat, I retched, unable to bring it up or send it down.

Evidently, I'd caused a real scene.

"Is she all right?"

"Give her the Heimlich!"

"No! Not yet. She can still breathe," Dave replied. He grabbed me by the shoulders and found my eyes with his.

"Em, relax, can you reach it in your mouth?" Dave asked steadily.

With his help, I calmed myself enough to reach into my mouth. Gagging, I was able to pull a long string from my throat and threw it onto the ground.

"Bloody hell! What is that?" Dave cried.

Between my feet rested what looked like thin, frayed cord covered in half-chewed cheese. Dave poked it with a stick.

"Oh dear, is that... I think that may be one of Astrid's dreadlocks."

As my mind made sense of the mess between my feet, I retched again.

The teenagers chimed in at high volume.

"Oooohhh, grosss!"

"Omigod, I'm gonna spew!"

Andrew enhanced the conversation with fake vomiting noises. He also planned to chase his new friends around the campsite with the regurgitated cheesy hair. Thankfully, his father intervened.

"Oh please. It's not like I did it on purpose. Don't be dickheads!" Astrid snapped at the children.

Astrid paused to scratch her leg and then chest before turning back to the stove.

6

The next morning, the group was allowed a slightly later start, leaving just after sunrise. A bit of morning light didn't make putting on my damp, now smelly wetsuit any more pleasant. Since we'd finished the majority of rapids, it would be a long day of paddling flat waters.

While rafts are designed for speed, resilience, and buoyancy in rivers, in open water it felt like paddling in an enormous chest of drawers. We made slow and grueling progress with already exhausted bodies. To make matters worse, there was a headwind.

To help pass the time Megan told us the fascinating story of Alexander Pearce—a true, 19th century, homoerotic tale of prison escape, murder, and cannibalism. She stretched the story out for over an hour, delighting me to distraction.

Meanwhile, Astrid had grown much quieter in the back, other than some unusually heavy breathing. Once, when I glanced back to take in the view, I noticed that Astrid's previously lean frame looked bloated, and her bulging body wobbled with each stroke. It was almost like something writhed inside her wetsuit, but at the time I dismissed this as boobs over forty.

She stared blankly ahead as she paddled, occasionally muttering something incoherent under her breath in German. She looked feverishly unwell, but at this point I was so tired of her mouth that I was just thankful so little came out of it.

Megan was more concerned.

"Astrid, I'm worried about you. I think we need to pull over, so I can examine you," Megan suggested.

"Piss off!" Astrid replied, scratching at the neck of her wetsuit. "I'm fine." She left long red claw marks in her flesh.

Megan frowned and then rolled her eyes, clearly finished helping Astrid. "Suit yourself," she sighed.

The itinerary called for a midday hiking detour through "The Lost World," a narrow muddy channel filled with slippery tree trunks and razor sharp rocks. Had we not condensed six days of paddling into three, our group might have had more stamina to enjoy the diversion. As it happened, Peter managed to sprain his ankle and Kate's shorts were literally ripped off her body after catching on a jagged limb as she fell. Slick as snail snot, it was perilously good, filthy fun. I would have enjoyed playing explorer more had I not been so shattered.

When we got back to the raft, Astrid was sleeping inside it. She had taken off her helmet to nap. Standing above her, I could see several angry raw spots on the crown of her head. It looked like her dreads had been pulled out in clumps and with it had come some of the surrounding flesh. Red and oozing, I thought back to my dinner from the night before and couldn't help but wonder about that meat in my quesadilla.

By this point Astrid's entire body looked swollen, the wetsuit cutting into her wrists and neck. She wheezed as she slept, puffing spittle from her cracking blue lips.

"We need to get her to a hospital! Where is that medicine kit?" Megan insisted, looking around for our trip leader Greg.

However, since we were the sweeping raft, the others had already loaded and left. They were a good ways downstream, along with the first aid bag. Worse still, Dave had stepped into the woods for a pee, so the gap widened significantly as we waited for him to shimmy out of and back into his damp wetsuit before returning.

"We'd have to paddle out regardless." I reasoned. "Let's push on."

Just then Astrid woke up.

"What in the hell are you doing, you idiots! The others are miles ahead of us. Get in the boat!" she screeched.

Astrid sort of swilled her way to her seat in the back, and like good little soldiers we filed in around her.

Those final hours on the Franklin River were three of the longest of my life. Moments after taking the helm, Astrid passed out again. Dave, Megan, and I compensated as best we could, changing positions so that Dave and Megan were up front, and I rode behind Megan on the right. We were three paddlers trying to catch up with boats being propelled by five people.

Ahead of us, the other rafts grew tiny and then disappeared. Still, we pushed on, knowing that the Gordon River would soon join ahead.

What felt like years later, we finally approached the confluence. From the back, we heard a noise.

Plip.

Plip, plop.

Plip, plop, ppppsssssssss.

"What was that?" Dave asked.

"Hold on, let me check," I turned and rose to my knees to peek back over the barrels at Astrid.

In the back, I saw Astrid slumped unnaturally over the side. Like a sack of rice, her right side seemed to be spilling into the water.

"Astrid! Are you okay?" I croaked.

Her bloodshot eyes opened, and she sloshed upright. Horrorstruck, I watched as leeches poured from an emptying arm of her wetsuit. Most went into the river, but as her weight transferred, some began dribbling into the raft.

WTF?

At this point, Astrid hissed and several leeches began to crawl out of her mouth! I watched, aghast, when one of her eyeballs plopped down her chest into the floorboard. A leech uncurled from the socket in her face.

Suddenly, Astrid's body lurched at me and tried to stand up, but inside her wetsuit her legs seemed to collapse at the hips. It was as if she no longer had bones, and the wetsuit was the only thing holding together a writhing, pulsing mass of leeches.

Survival kicked in. I jumped onto the barrels between us and used my paddle, the T-grip, to jab the disintegrating body back. Its torso flopped backwards out of the boat, but the legs remained on the floorboard. The wetsuit kept the body suspended, half in and out of the raft. Down in the footwell, leeches began to wiggle out of Astrid's hollowing river booties.

Thinking fast, I used the paddle again, this time to flip one of the legs over the back. As the balance shifted, the rest of Astrid's body slid out of the boat and began sinking into the water. However, hundreds of leeches had filled the floorboard.

Together they rose and stretched their bodies, like seaweed, reaching toward me. In unison they let out a long slow hiss. Then, they began advancing in my direction.

Now what? I was out of ideas.

Abruptly, the boat took a sharp turn right, and I fell to my knees on the barrels as the current of the Gordon grabbed our raft. As our boat turned, I looked down to realize in amazement that the leeches had paused. The mass seemed confused, and several had started inching away from me, over the back bumper of the raft, into the water. By this time our raft was almost entirely into the Gordon River. Suddenly, I understood.

"All Forward!" I shouted. "Paddle! Paddle! Paddle!"

Dave and Megan jumped into action, quickly propelling our raft fully into the safety of the Gordon River. As our raft left the current of the magical Franklin River, a final leech slipped over the side returning to its home.

Plip.

We knew that the next morning, a private yacht would shuttle our group six hours upstream, back to civilization. After five days in the wild, we were all looking forward to a hot shower. Anticipation fueled our filthy, weary bodies.

We rode dusk into darkness on the Gordon River. Into blackness, ripples reflected the moonlight from above as we quietly paddled toward our final campsite. I felt a deep peace and satisfaction in the softness of night. It was the perfect ending to another grand adventure.

Eventually, we caught up with the others.

"We lost you guys back there. Where's Astrid?" Greg asked, concern for his wife creeping into his voice.

Dave, Megan, and I all looked at each other, unsure of how to begin.

"Well, it's difficult to explain," Dave started.

"And strange. So strange that it's hard to believe," Megan added.

"Actually, it's almost like a science fiction story," I explained.

SHAME MARATHON

Lisbon, Portugal, 2004

Sixteen years ago, I ran a marathon in Lisbon, Portugal. I trained for over four months, but on the big day *I didn't do as well as I'd hoped.* That's what I always tell people, if I tell people, when the topic of marathon running comes up: *"I ran a marathon once, but I didn't do as well as I'd hoped."* More often than not, in those conversations I stay quiet instead because the truth of that day is so much worse. To be completely honest, on that long day nearly two decades ago, I came in last place.

"Well, *at least I wasn't last!*" people always laugh after competitions, with relief. Well, folks, I'm here to tell you, somebody was.

There were a few factors that contributed to my poor performance. *"Oh here we go. Of course you have excuses; Losers always have excuses,"* Astrid, my inner bully, joins in. For starters, the marathon wasn't even my idea. Sure, I prided myself on being sporty, on having been a Division One

165

student-athlete in college, but at the time, I think the farthest I'd ever run, just for the sake of running, was maybe four or five miles.

Don't be fooled, people.
Ol' Amy Wambach here quit university soccer after a year and half.

By the time I was 28, I had softened back into average shape. Back then, a coworker, who was full of hot-but-inspiring air, convinced me and a group of other young friends that we could all run a marathon. "By the time you've trained for a half, you've practically trained for a full," Maggie had said. We lived in Germany at the time, and she'd found the (relatively) nearby 2004 Lisbon Marathon online, which would be a perfect goal—a flat, fast, beautiful course. We planned to use a training schedule from a runner's magazine to lead up to the big event. Bright-eyed and motivated, our fun little group started running together, for about two weeks. But, very quickly into the training program, one by one, Maggie and everyone else dropped out.

Boo hoo, cry baby. Get on with the story.

I trained alone in the Alps, on mountain trails in the snow, for four months. My pace was very slow because I had to move carefully along the slick outdoor paths. I averaged 11- to 12-minute miles. I hoped to run my marathon in 4 hours and 30 minutes.

Are you kidding me, Grandma? WEAK.
Astrid, Stop.

When it was time for the marathon, my (ex) husband and I flew to Lisbon. At registration, I picked up my runner's number and a race package of assorted details. Inside was a free ticket to a buffet dinner, hosted by a sponsoring hotel. *Sweet!* The race volunteer explained that the meal tickets ran in three shifts and that I had the last shift, a late one at 8 p.m. However, several hours later when we arrived, a flustered waitress explained that the buffet had already run out of food. It seemed that the chef hadn't considered how carb-loading marathon runners would eat probably two to three times the amount of normal dinner guests.

We were told that more food was coming, so I picked at my pickles and olives from a decimated salad bar as we waited, for over an hour. To my memory, once or twice, a manic chef brought out a large, steaming pot of plain spaghetti noodles (all the sauce was finished), and he was immediately set upon by a flock of angry, starving marathoners (mostly men) who elbowed in for a few scraps from the bowl. Many had been waiting since the second dinner shift.

By this time it was close to 9:30 p.m., and while I worried that other restaurants in town would be closing, we decided to try our luck elsewhere. Since we didn't know the town and couldn't speak the language, it didn't go well. In the end, I ate snacks, chips and candy bars from a convenience store, for my pre-marathon dinner. I had cold toast from a sad little continental breakfast bar the next morning.

Why weren't you more prepared? At the very least, you could have waited and elbowed into that crowd at the dinner buffet. Okay, so you didn't speak Portuguese, and you're "shy," whatever that means. Why didn't you advocate for yourself? You should have tried harder. Bottom line, 28 is fully-grown, Amy, but you acted like a child.

I remember that the morning of the race was a cold one. I didn't warm up for exercise because I was so cold at the starting line that I just curled into a ball until it was time. I figured I had four-and-a-half hours to "warm up," and at 28 years old, I wasn't wrong.

Stretching is for pussies!
Jesus, Astrid.

Don't bring Jesus into this.
What would your beloved grandmother say
If she heard you talking this way?
She'd say "Amy, Jesus is already a part of this. Honey, please, just open
your heart to him.

Oh sure. In other words, Repent!
Or, join all your non-Christian and LGBTQ+ friends to
BURN IN HELL, honey.

I remember the crowd at the starting line. I have come to understand that there were just over 200 full-marathoners that day, 13 of which were women, but I didn't know that at the time. There were also tons of people running the half-marathon and other shorter distances, but overall, it was a relatively small race. To me, it seemed like an enormous crowd that wrapped all the way around a stadium track and even a little beyond, but I would later learn that my race was tiny when compared to the major marathons of the world. Regardless, I can still feel the hum of that starting line, that jittery energy of thousands gathered together before a race. Looking back after 16 years, the memory of that human buzz drowns out any "*BANG!*" of a starting gun.

The next thing I distinctly remember, maybe three miles into the race, was...

Surprise surprise, needing to use the toilet, again. Of course, I had used the facilities numerous times before the race. *-And Astrid, before you get started, I know you hate being one of those humans that needs to pee often, but get over it, already. You've seen our mother. It's only going to get worse.*

As I jogged along, I debated my strategy of how/ where/ when to go, so that when I finally saw a single porta-potty up ahead, I decided to make a pit stop. Outside of the portable toilet, a race volunteer was waiting her turn.

She said, "There is someone inside, and I have been waiting. But, since you are a runner, please, you go ahead." She gave up and walked away.

I thanked the woman as she headed off, and tried to be patient as I bounced outside the toilet door. I was trying to make noise to alert the person inside that I was serious. All the while, hundreds of runners streamed past, and I grew increasingly desperate, both physically and mentally. It was probably only five minutes at most, but it felt like hours. Eventually, I tried to open the door, only to realize that no one was inside the toilet.

Why are you always so worried about being polite?
You should have knocked sooner.
It's your own fault.
Dumbass.

After using the toilet, I got back on track. There were still plenty of runners in the pack, and I found my stride. Recently, I've read that the Lisbon Marathon is one of the most beautiful in the world, but I can't remember the course. I recall running seaside, along main roads, and I remember running up what seemed like a massive freeway at one point. It felt strange to run along those major streets, minus the cars, of course, like the world had come to an end.

I was having another little issue, too.

It's like living inside a goldfish, folks.

My pacing. As an American, I was raised to think in miles. Meanwhile, the rest of the world got-with-the-program long ago. Portugal used kilometers. I'd asked Maggie, my resident marathon expert, about it, and she assured me that since it was an international race, all distances would be posted in both kilometers and miles. As it turned out, Maggie was an ignorant slut.

How is this Maggie's fault? You shouldn't have relied on her.
Also, don't say "slut." It's shaming.
Ya' dipshit.

Anyway, in the US, we strangely refer to our shorter-distance running events in kilometers, 5k runs and 10k runs. I'm not sure why, but I think because it sounds fancy. I knew, for example, that a 10k race was 6.2 miles because, as a child, I had proudly watched my dad run the "Cowtown 10k" in Fort Worth, Texas. However, beyond 10 kilometers, Americans switch back to thinking in miles. These days, most Americans who know about running understand a half marathon to be 13.1 miles, and we think of a full marathon as 26.2 miles.

So there I was on race day, fighting for my life, and also having to do math. For example, at the 18-kilometer marker, I'm sure I thought, *Well, hell. Okay, 18k is not quite 20k, so not quite 12 miles. Maybe 10-ish. I've run about ten miles, which means I have about 16 more miles to go, I think.* And so it went. Now, for those of you wondering, I know this answer from a personal learning experience: the full distance of a 26.2-mile marathon in kilometers is 42. Forty. Fucking. Two. Kilometers.

Despite a few hurdles, the first half of my marathon, overall, was positive. If my day had stopped there, the experience would have left me with a very different, self-affirming memory. I ran 13.1 miles/21 kilometers, at my pace, in a pack of runners, to a cheering crowd. If I'd signed up for the half instead, I would have been really proud of myself. If I still had the knees for it, I'd even consider doing that again one day.

But you don't have the knees for it. Get over it.
True, Astrid. My running days are behind me now,
And it still makes us sad.

Anyway, back when I *could* run, as I passed the channel leading to the half-marathon finishers' gate, about two-and-a-half hours into our race, the crowd of runners thinned dramatically. Suddenly, there were very few of us left on the road. We were the full marathoners. It was then that I realized how much my bathroom mishap had cost me. Other than a handful of other runners, who would eventually leave me behind or pass me up, I was alone—running and doing math with Astrid.

Looking back, the second half of my marathon was a bit like one of my all-time favorite movies *Fight Club* (a 1999 American film with director David Fincher, starring Brad Pitt, Edward Norton, and Helena Bonham Carter). For those of you who haven't seen it, I won't ruin it. However, on my marathon day so long ago, not unlike Edward Norton's character, I was beating the shit out of myself.

> *I guess that makes me Brad Pitt.*
> *Shut up.*

It didn't take long for me to realize I was going to be one of the last finishers. Out of fuel, I knew it was bad when a man in his 60s, a Asian American, left me in his dust. And later, a grandmother in her 70s, somebody's great white Nana, zipped past me as well. Still, I never stopped running. *(Actually, I walked for 10 to 20 steps in order to stabilize my hand enough to drink through a few water stops, but otherwise, I ran the entire 26.2 miles.)* I was alone for last two hours of the race, trying not to think about the marathon crew that patiently swept up behind me.

With a captive audience, Astrid took this opportunity to say a few words, between bloody punches into my loosening teeth and kicks to my snapping ribs.

> *Last place! How could you let this happen?*
> *You aren't just a loser. You are THE LOSER.*

> *Not only are you a terrible wife and a terrible woman,*
> *You are a terrible person.*

You'll always be an outsider because you don't belong anywhere.
People don't like you because you aren't likable.
You make everyone uncomfortable.

You aren't built to be happy.
You don't deserve to be.

It's probably for the best you haven't had children.
You shouldn't reproduce.

About this time, somewhere between 17 and 23 miles into my marathon (I can't be mathematically certain), a Portuguese motorcycle policeman pulled up and asked me for my phone number. He thought I was cute. I hoped he would lose control and crash his motorbike. (Not horrifically, mind you. Just enough to crush, bruise, and pin him to the ground while I made a snail's escape.)

I'd tied my long sleeve t-shirt from that cold morning around my waist, so I was running in a sports bra and spandex shorts. Astrid tells me I was dressed too provocatively, and that I was probably asking for it.

It's okay to call yourself a slut.

Anywho, I'd like to offer a little advice to those out there who might need to hear it. Folks, fellas, let me just say that flirting with the last runner in a marathon is a bit like hunting for ladies in the hospital maternity ward. Even though you can catch 'em, I'd suggest you just leave 'em for another day. Boys, the chances of getting a date are *real* slim.

Of course, I didn't realize what was actually happening inside me, at the time of the marathon. I mean, I just thought I was "pushing myself." It wasn't until nine years later, when I began a spotty meditation practice in 2013 that

I would come to realize that Astrid lived in my head. It turned out that *she* was that brutal voice inside who likes to stab me in the kidneys, despite her machine gun spray of rainbows to the rest of humanity. And it wasn't until my 2018 Tasmanian rafting trip, when I met someone so nasty (bless her heart) that I was inspired to give my Astrid a name. So you can imagine my surprise when, just this year, it was revealed to me that my Astrid is also German, just like her namesake! I had no idea; she doesn't even have an accent! (However, she now occasionally speaks to me like an American doing a terrible impression of a German.) At any rate, these days sweet little Astrid is always there, never far below my surface, stabbing organs for fun. Once I found her and named her, I decided there was really only thing left to do: love her.

A thousand years later, at some point the signs began to count down to the finish line. I slipped my long sleeve T-shirt back on, in an attempt to block any extra rays of unwanted attention. It was like putting on sunscreen to fly directly into a star.

At the "7 km" marker I was relieved because it seemed pretty close, but I was beyond doing the required computation. By this time, even Astrid was tired, and my whole being had gone numb. Only now, in retrospect as a writer, am I able to see all the people on the streets, those who actually did turn to cheer me through the finish—those who paused in their daily errands to turn and clap and cheer for that final young woman who never gave up. Instead, for years, I have only replayed the words of one jerk on that last stretch. He made fun of me in English so that I was sure to understand.

"Look at her go," he shouted to his friends. "Is she the first one or the last one?"

They all roared at his cruel joke. I wouldn't have thought it possible to feel any worse. It was.

But I kept running.

Otherwise, looking back, I can see now that there was so much kindness being sent my way. *Thank you, Lisbon.* Unfortunately, I was beyond receiving it at the time.

By the time I crossed the finish line, I was an open wound. There at the final gates, my body crashed to the ground, and I started sobbing. My devastation was naked, so lurid and raw it was too much to witness. Most people averted their eyes as I wept. My first husband (who was a good guy, just not the right guy) lifted me up and helped me move out of the way. Around me, race volunteers busily packed up what remained of the event. After all, it had been a long day for everyone.

And, there you have it. That's the story of my Lisbon marathon. *What a hoot, right?*

Amy, I'm not trying to be mean, but face it. You were young and healthy with no excuses. You had clearly underprepared. They needed to open the roads, and everyone had been waiting for you, the very last runner, for almost six hours. People had lives to get on with. Afterward, yet again in life, your uncontrolled emotional intensity just made everyone else uncomfortable. You weren't a victim in this story or any other. The only difficulty you've known in your charmed little life is all the bullshit you've put yourself and others through. Even my "abuse" is just a twisted luxury of your own self-indulgence. Toughen up, Princess, and quit looking for sympathy. IT'S NOT ALWAYS ABOUT YOU!

Astrid, you have a point. A lot of what you're saying is true, and I'm working on it. But I also know now that it was okay for me back then to feel heartbroken. I don't want sympathy, but I'd welcome a little empathy. Of course, I was shattered. I'd been running for six hours on a belly of cheese puffs! Astrid, darling, I know you're scared, but for once in our life, who cares what all the people are thinking. Oh, and I'm not trying to be mean, but here's a message to all the hateful little trolls out there:

Up Yours.

I deserve to be proud of running that marathon.

Believe it or not, as I've grown older I've grown kinder, both to others and myself. *(I know, thank you. We clearly have more work to do.)* Maybe I'm a late bloomer, but in my early 40s, I'm only just beginning to understand something crucial. Looking back, it's easier now to have compassion for my 28-year-old self in Lisbon, that girl who gave a marathon what little and everything she had. I happened to be the "worst" runner that day, but I gave it my best shot. The only person I hurt *(and boy-howdy did it hurt)* was myself. And yet, for years, I've been quietly ashamed of that tenacious young woman.

It's much harder to have compassion for myself when I wasn't at my best—for the times when I hurt *(and boy-howdy did I hurt)* a precious few. My younger self, especially, was miles from perfect. At times, she thoughtlessly splashed through muddy puddles, but she also deliberately stomped through heaping piles of cow shit and then skid across living room carpets.

I wonder how many of us are still punishing ourselves for our unforgivable actions from years and years ago—those hateful words to a loved one, a chapter of promiscuity, or some personal version of a car crash. The deceptions, the divorces, the addictions, the abortions, fill in the blank with your unpardonable crimes. *"**You don't deserve forgiveness**,"* some people will say, and they are allowed to see it that way.

But here's the thing: "they," and those who actually do matter, may never forgive me, but I have to. I am the only person responsible for my feelings of worth, and my regrets don't make me worthless. There will always be someone who doesn't like me or doesn't get me, or who won't give me the benefit of the doubt, but I can try to do that for myself and other people.

I also know there are those who can never forgive me for my sins— that if others knew my secrets, they might accept me, but they'd no longer respect me. I have to let that go, too, because I'm tired. My life is half over, and I can't afford to waste any more time. Ultimately, I'm the only one that has to live with me, I mean, besides good ol' Astrid, who—by the way, I'm proud to say—is finally finishing up that 2004 Lisbon Marathon.

So, for those of you who have ever come in last in a marathon, I see you. You are my people. No matter what, we did it!

And for those of you who are still punishing yourselves for events that happened years and years ago, I see you too, and you're welcome to come jog with me. Actually, I'm a walker these days, and a bit of a rambler, but please know that you aren't alone.

I think, perhaps, we aren't meant to run our shame marathons forever. I invite you all to join me at a finish line, but only if you would like to come and only when you're ready. Please put your hands together, and let's cheer each other on.

Congratulations! <u>Astrid</u>! You made it!

The 2004 Lisbon Marathon

Race time: <u>16 years, 2 months, 1 week, 3 days, 5 hours and 47 minutes.</u>

Author's note: Please don't worry about us, folks. Now that we're in our 40s, Astrid and I are much kinder to eachother. We've come a long way. Almost two decades later, I can understand why Astrid has been so defensive about that race. In a way, it's even a little bit funny. When I registered for the race, I lived in Germany, so my race tag said I was German, not American. I think one reason why my little fräulein was so ashamed for all those years is because official records will show that the very last finisher of the 2004 Lisbon Marathon was a German woman.

NO REGRETS

Brazil, 2016

Some people claim to have no regrets in life because they "wouldn't be where they are today without those experiences." Oh please. Clearly those people weren't applying themselves. Personally, I have a mental medicine cabinet crammed full of sticky bad choices, a range of reminders of stinging abrasions to tingling amputations. Inside are sharp, bitter little lozenges that I select from and tongue absentmindedly. Without realizing it, I might pop in my "Teenage Boyfriend Regret," and before I know it I've moved onto my "Hip-thrusting a Colleague at the Christmas Party Regret."

My screw-ups come in a variety of strengths and flavors, but most I have sucked down into thin, light discs that I can easily snap into digestible slivers. Others remain thick, grooved, and cloyingly mentholated, despite decades of nursing. With time, practice, and some self-compassion, I'm learning how to gently spit those out, shut the bathroom door, and go back into the living room. I repeat as often as needed, which—mercifully with time—seems to be less and less.

I got my first tattoo in 1999 when I was 22 years old. It was taken from a hand-sized, oval, Mexican beach pebble with the word "Joy" carved on one side and four Precambrian-like dancing women on the other. I bought the stone from a boutique in downtown Fort Worth, Texas. I wish I'd taken note of the artist, but it didn't occur to me in those days.

I wanted my tattoo to have profound meaning, and "Joy" was a concept I had discussed at length with an older friend and spiritual mentor. "Joy is fiercer than happiness," she said. "Joy has an intensity that can be double-edged, reckless even. Children bring joy, but they can also break your heart. It's healthy to cultivate what brings us happiness, but be mindful of Joy. It sparkles and fades. When you feel it, be sure to cherish it."

So, after much tattoo deliberation, when I finally saw that unique river stone resting in a shop window, it whispered to me, "Amy, I'm super deep. You should go get me tattooed on your lower back, centered right above your ass." And, with just the right amount of peer pressure from a rubbernecked friend, I drove to the nearest tattoo shop and got it done. I wish I'd taken note of that artist, too, but I was too oblivious to care.

Astonishingly, I've never regretted that tattoo. It's a snapshot of who I was at that time in my life, and that seeking, reckless, fierce young woman could have done much worse. I'm thankful to both artists because it is a solid rendering of a beautiful, original image—one that I occasionally wish I could see more easily, without having to contort in front of the mirror like a circus entertainer.

Seventeen years went by before I got my next tattoo in São Paulo, Brazil.

In 2016, Carlos Silva was considered by many as one of the "Top Watercolor Tattooists in the World." His work was admired not only by tattoo enthusiasts, but also by many artists in the tattoo industry. As an expert in his field, he maintained a fully-booked appointment schedule with a long wait list, and he even offered training seminars to other artists. In other words, clients didn't choose Carlos; Carlos chose his clients.

I knew about Carlos because I'd been sucked down an Internet rabbit hole. I'd always appreciated women with bold yet tasteful tattoos. I admired those who'd had the courage and artistic vision to have it done right and well. From the safety of my sofa, I found myself playing with ideas, researching tattoos to learn about different artists and styles. The techniques and talent I found amazed me. Sure, like everyone, I knew that tattoos could be bad, really *really* bad. However, over a period of several months, I began to recognize the difference between good tattoos, great tattoos, and the work of masters.

Carlos Silva was a master. Of the dozens of top tattoo artists I more deeply researched, his style was my favorite. Carlos became my dream artist so I sent him an email. *Why the hell not*, I figured, and fired a message off. I was shocked when Carlos actually replied several months later. We both used Google Translate to communicate. Folks, *this excrement immediately became authentic.*

We set an appointment for eight months later.

A childhood friend named Jennifer recently said to me, "I'll never get a tattoo. I know it's terrible of me, but I can't help but think they make people look trashy. Plus, I just imagine it aging in fast-forward, sped up in some horrible time-lapse video."

Jenn laughed at her own cleverness, and, I'll admit, the video part was funny. However, she didn't realize that I had tattoos of my own, a new one hiding just under my shirtsleeve. There was a difference between having a preference and feeling superior. To me, Jennifer's self-righteous tone was much uglier than any my dark mark of mine.

I wasn't surprised how Jenn felt about tattoos, only that she'd actually said it. Through the years, our worldviews had grown increasingly apart, each of us with a different take on politics and religion—or so I gathered from social media. *Funny how the tools designed to bring people together are so good at turning us against one another.* I assumed that Jenn and I didn't see eye-to-eye about much anyone, but she was still a person I cared about. I knew she was conservative, so I'd worn long sleeves for a reason that day—to play nice and avoid the subject; however, the topic of tattoos came up when a decorated person walked by.

Screw it. I decided to let my friend really see me.

"Well, I guess you'd better take a look at this then," I said, pushing up my cuff to flash my new ink.

Jenn's face fell and turned pink when she realized her gaff.

"Oh Amy. I'm sorry. I didn't know."

"Meh. Don't worry, Jenn. I have three. Besides, is a fading tattoo really any worse than imagining our entire bodies aging in a fast-forward, time-lapse video?" I joked.

We took a moment to visualize our bodies quickly swelling with middle-aged weight and then shriveling and sagging into 85-year-old birthday suits. We shook our heads, shuddered, and cackled. Two imperfect human beings, my old friend and I laughed ourselves to tears.

Afterwards, Jennifer wiped her eyes. She grabbed my arm, took a close look, and smiled.

"Amy, it's beautiful."

One might presume that the problem with setting an appointment date with the tattoo artist of your dreams, or even with the tattoo artist down the street, is deciding what you forever want on your slowly-deteriorating body. Valid. However, in my research, I'd learned that tattoo artists in the top tiers usually designed their own creative content. This meant that those lucky enough to get an appointment were often required to select from the artist's images, samples first sketched or painted by the artist. Clients were simply canvases.

By this stage I was very familiar with Carlos's remarkable portfolio. I knew I'd end up with a unique design, an original that would only be tattooed on me. I was prepared to choose from the options Carlos offered me. *Hmm, I guess I'll take The Hulk.* Actually, I thought his best work was of wildlife, birds and other animals, and I admired it all. Worst-case scenario, I was primed to be awkward, which was one of my strengths. I could always say 'No, thank you," tip Carlos generously for his time, and walk away. It was my body after all. I felt very confident, however, that I'd love whatever new content he was working on.

I was both delighted and paralyzed when Carlos asked me in an email what I wanted.

Dave and I rarely eat at fast food chains, unless we're traveling. I can't justify it, except to say that sometimes when everything around you is new and strange, the consistent comfort of a consumable hockey puck is reassuring. Also, when we can't speak the local language, Dave can always hold up his fingers to indicate that we want two "Number Ones," which can become surprisingly confusing. Too shy and hangry to bungle through the order myself, I hide behind Dave and burst out with clarifying comments once he screws it all up. It's a wonder he stays married to me.

This is how we spent our first evening in São Paulo, Brazil—in the food court, at the mall across the street from our hotel. That afternoon we had explored the neighborhood on foot to find the tattoo shop in advance. We were all set and waiting for the big appointment.

People-watching is one of my favorite pastimes, and the mall in Brazil was fruitful. I knew my over-generalizing, historically misguided impressions were probably inaccurate, but I learned best through experience and fine-tuned accordingly. In Brazil, I wondered if I might see the world's most gorgeous women, those who aren't against a little surgical boost. Perhaps I'd recognize descendants of Amazon women, from the Amazon river, enormous warriors who were now experts in that dancy martial art called "caipirinha." If any passed by that night, it wasn't obvious to me.

Instead, I remember being surprised by how tall the men were and by how disappointingly, well, average the women were. While I've never been particularly fashionable, I took note of the Brazilian trends that year. That night in the mall, women of all ages wore low-waisted, boom-boom jeans that highlighted their asset. Big eyeglasses, like those worn in the 1970s disco decade in the USA, were also common. An incredibly diverse place, as expected in the world's eleventh most populous city, there were all sorts of people. However, I was surprised to see that relatively few folks had tattoos. That night we hung out in the mall like teenagers, slowly counting down to my tattoo appointment. Killing time was killing me.

The following afternoon, my interpreter Paul, whom I hadn't met before, was waiting for us outside the tattoo studio (I was fortunate to have friends living in São Paulo that year who introduced us online). Paul had graduated high school that summer. How odd it must have been for him to take a middle-aged couple, teachers his parents' age, to get the wife a tattoo. I briefly battled a mothering voice inside me. *Paul, I want you to understand that I'm well established in my career, and that I've done years of research to find an excellent tattoo artist. Please listen to what I say as you watch what I'm about to do: think long and hard before you get a tattoo, especially one that you can't easily hide.* It was boggling that I could be both my mother and a tattooed lady. Who was I becoming? In the end I kept my mouth shut, confident that like most 18-year-olds, Paul already had his own parents to completely ignore.

Inside the shop, the receptionist Alice was pleased to see us. She introduced us to Carlos, whom I recognized from the Internet. They both seemed very relieved that I'd brought Paul to translate, and Carlos later admitted that he'd moaned at Alice for booking an appointment with an English-speaking client. Evidently, they each thought the other had a better command of the language, and they'd been worried about my appointment.

Carlos was tall, in his early 30s, and covered in tattoos. His dark hair, eyes, mustache and goatee complimented a very kind, bright smile. He was handsome and baby-faced. And so incredibly talented.

Filtered through Paul, Carlos started by referring to the email I had sent months earlier, in which I described my idea. I had decided on two small birds, firefinches, from Ethiopia where I was then living. These tiny, adorable red and brown birds lived and played in the alleyways near my home.

I mustered my courage. If I had the opportunity to get a tattoo from one of the world's best, then *I sure as heck was gonna show that sucker off*. I had decided on my inner forearm for the bright red male. I thought the female would look nice peeking from behind my shoulder. Her shyness paired with his flash would mimic their natural behavior. I explained my idea to Carlos, but I asked what he thought would look best. After all, he was the virtuoso.

In addition to the photos I'd sent by email, Carlos pulled up several images online. He gathered his thoughts for 10 to 15 minutes, and then we sat down to get started. Using the tattoo machine, Carlos freehanded the first tattoo, the male finch, directly onto my arm. It barely hurt as the bird took shape, just a small stinging sensation. I had prepared myself to sit for hours, but it only took about 30 minutes to complete. We went through the same process for the female. She took a few minutes longer to finish and stung just a bit more. Both birds turned out fantastically—ready to take flight off of my body.

I was fascinated by Carlos's creative process, eager to see how one of the world's best artists harnessed *the ether*. When I think back to that day what I remember most was ease. Carlos plainly enjoyed his colleagues and laughed effortlessly with them and us as he worked. He seemed to surround himself with positive people, those who made him feel comfortable and unhindered. Also, I felt connected to Carlos—like he understood what I was looking for and that in another context we might have been friends. From one artist to another, I trusted him and treasured his gift. In exchange, he marked me with magic.

I still have the impulse to attach deep meaning to my tattoos, and my newest tattoos do serve as personal reminders of places, people, and concepts. However, mostly, when I catch a glimpse of these beautiful birds I feel happy, which is something I've heard is healthy to cultivate in life.

We turned the trip into a two-week vacation. Brazil is an enormous country, and we only pricked its skin. We spent time in the two nearest major cities, São Paulo and Rio. It was two months before the Olympics, and we were able to witness them set up in Rio. We also made time for the charming, cobblestone, old gold town of Paraty. Nearby, we managed to avoid the Zika virus as we relaxed in a jungle hostel. One day we hiked up Sugarloaf Peak to view Brazil's only tropical fjord, Saco do Mamanguá. Finally, we took a flight down to the Argentinian border to see one of the world's most powerful waterfalls, the magnificent Iguazu Falls.

Old photographs of the trip help freeze the blur into isolated memories. I see the two of us standing in front of the Christ the Redeemer statue, Jesus' enormous arms spreading wide over the city of Rio behind us. There are shots of our feet in hiking boots, overlooking an aquamarine fjord. There's another one with our hair soaked after riding a speedboat into the thundering mist of one of the Great Natural Wonders of the World. The photos feature Dave and me, off exploring together, just snapshots of a place and time in our lives.

Somehow, I always manage to find room for old sorrows on my journey. I fill my backpack with the essentials: a down jacket and sleeping bag, extra layers, and a small bar of soap for my alternate pairs of underwear and socks. I pack cashews, sunscreen, iodine, and duct tape for blisters. I carefully check and recheck my pack for unnecessary bulk, calculating that water weighs 2.2 lbs per liter. I wonder how much regret weighs.

It's no longer a surprise to find I've included my insulted ego, half a dozen misunderstandings, an old jar of pickled rejections and several re-crumpled choices. I always find room for that broken friendship, some divorce rubble, and my trusty pet cat o' nine tails. Sometimes, as I hike along, I pull out and fiddle with a keepsake from this painful collection, until I realize what I'm doing. I have to remind myself, "That's enough, Amy. Let it go."

Again and again, as I travel through the overwhelming beauty of this planet, I release old heartaches with love. I repeat this as often as needed, which has been both often and needed. With mercy and time, it seems to be less. I doubt my pack will ever be empty, but little by little, I am learning what to do with the weight. I'm also learning to step more carefully, and I'm discovering how to be kinder to myself. After all, my life has been glittered with joy, and there is so much to cherish along the way.

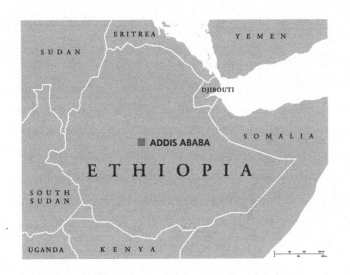

CHICKEN DANCE

Ethiopia, 2014–2017

I love the all-staff parties at Bonnie and Clyde's house. Those two throw amazing, albeit notorious, gatherings. With an outdoor dance floor, DJ, fire pit, a medieval buffet, and ga-ga-gallons of alcohol, they don't mess around. I always look forward to their parties in anticipation, and then backwards in pain.

Upon arrival, just after work ends at 4:31 in the afternoon, a compulsory tequila shot grants entrance to the party. Then, if you are still standing near the gate as other guests arrive, you are required to take another shot with the new group. Clyde, who is also my boss, enforces this rule and pours the shots. Since I don't want to be accused of not being a team player, of course I drink, and then I loiter near the entryway. I think it's a fabulous company policy; however, let the record show that those that don't wish to partake just take a wide berth at the entrance gate, and rides home are always provided. It's all in good fun.

The best part about these gatherings is the crowd. It is one of a few work occasions where locals (Habesha) and foreigners (Farenj) mix socially. Everyone loosens up and lets their hair down. You should see the dance floor—talk about cultural connections. The music jumps between queens, from America's Beyoncé to Ethiopia's Betty G. Covering Ethio-jazz, rap, modern, and traditional, the best DJs can bring together people, places, styles, and generations. At any party, especially a cross-cultural one, the dance floor is my favorite place to be.

Ethiopians love to dance. So do I. My friends of all colors will tell you I'm a good dancer, and not just "for a white girl," thank you very much. I love to shake my bootie; however, I have trouble with Ethiopian dancing because it's all in the shoulders. Sure, I can "shimmy," but this isn't that. Ethiopian shoulder-dancing, called "eskista," is more of a controlled, rhythmic popping that involves the whole torso. The men add jumping and circling the room. Meanwhile, Ethiopian women include their necks and chests, making it look effortless and so graceful, almost birdlike. Full of liquid courage, we Westerners try to eskista and end up looking like birds too, but more like chickens—with their necks wrung. I call it the Death Flap.

Beyond my peers at parties, there are professional dancers in Ethiopia who mesmerize audiences with visual storytelling. A cherished art form in the community, dance troupes are often hired for big events like weddings or conferences, but there are also smaller cultural restaurants that are popular among tourists and locals alike. These venues offer sublime local cuisine, and they put on classic dance shows.

There are several traditional folk dances, and many seem to involve the harvest and finding a mate. The men and women take turns. There are often costume changes during a performance, but you will usually see women in brightly embroidered, white cotton dresses. It's also common for men to change into green shorts outfits that are covered in big, white buttons. To me, the dances seem to be a flirtation between men and women before they join together at the end. Finally, the entertainers go into the audience to encourage overly sober people to get up and dance. Delight turns to dread, vicarious embarassment, as we all watch white, middle-aged accountants get pulled up onto the stage.

Of the many dances, one of the most impressive is the Ethiopian head spinning dance. In this performance, a talented, brave young woman of supple spine whips her head around and around and around at blurring speeds. It's amazing and distressing to watch, a technique that I'm sure takes years of practice, but not *too* many years.

The head dance is something I would have tried when I was younger, back before my joints began snapping off and flaking into crumbly chunks. These days, I'm pretty sure I would just break my neck. On the plus side, I suppose that'd be a good starting place for my death flap.

New Zealand

NEW ZEALAND

Great Barrier Island

North Island

WELLINGTON

Banks Peninsula

South Island

Otago Peninsula

Stewart Island

EIGHT AND TWO
HALF-TRAMPS

New Zealand, 2017

FUUUUUDGE! I shrieked inside my head. (I didn't think "fudge.")

The pain I felt was not the chronic knee pain that I had grown used to. I already suspected that my joints were actually made of peppermint candy rather than bone, cracking off and snapping off into bite-size little chunks. I'd learned to suck on, to suck up that kind of pain. But this wasn't peppermint pain. This injury was sharper, making me wince with each downhill step. This new sensation—this was lightning lemon pain.

Surely, this was not what New Zealanders meant by "sweet-as."

The Americans called it "hiking." In South Africa, we had gone "trekking." Britons preferred an understated "walking." But by far, my favorite term for bipedaling outdoors came from the Kiwis. In New Zealand, they called it "tramping."

I began my travel research almost a year in advance by searching online for the "Best Hikes in New Zealand." From there I quickly discovered the governmental Department of Conservation (DOC) website. Bingo! I perked up as the page described "New Zealand's Nine Great Walks":

"Take a walk, a Great Walk, through some of New Zealand's most awe-inspiring landscapes on premier walking tracks…New Zealand's nine Great Walks are premier tracks that pass through diverse and spectacular scenery. From native forests, lakes and rivers to rugged mountain peaks, deep gorges and vast valleys…there's a Great Walk for everyone!"

I quickly learned that New Zealand was a tramper's paradise. Beyond the Great Nine, which were multi-day, hut-to-hut hikes designed to capture the best of New Zealand's North and South Islands, the country had hundreds of other shorter walks and day hikes. With over 950 overnight huts, numerous tent campgrounds, and rangers who looked after the trails and the tourists, New Zealand made it easy for people to get outside.

I also learned that the Great Walk huts book up quickly, especially the Milford Track, which was regarded as one of the world's finest walks. Typically, its entire season sold out in less than a week. Registration for all walks opened six months early, so I would need to have my act together in order to get us spots.

Our plan was to visit New Zealand for five months because, if you're going all that way, you might as well do it right. I approached the Great Walks with a similar rationale.

What the heck, I thought. *Let's do them all.*

The North Island

"Well, *gggrreat.*" I grumbled like an upset Tony the Tiger, and bent my knees to brace my feet up on the dashboard.

I made it clear that I was frustrated.

"I beg your pardon?" Dave asked cautiously, avoiding eye contact with me.

We were on the road, north of Auckland, New Zealand. We'd only been in our new van for two hours.

"This seat!" I huffed. "It's giving me scoliosis. Look."

To illustrate, I put my feet down and let go of the internal 'oh shit' handle. My body slumped halfway into the floorboard. The springs had (evidently) sprung, and the left hand seat melted toward the door.

"Oh dear. Why didn't you say something before we bought it?" Dave asked.

I took a moment to simply glare at him, Captain Obvious. We'd thoroughly examined the back of the van before our purchase, but clearly I'd forgotten to consider my comfort in the front. And why was this my fault? There was no need to rub my nose in it.

"Sir, would you like a punch before lunch?"

In our little family of two, we liked to threaten each other with violence before the midday meal.

"I'm fine, thank you. Perhaps when we stop later to shop for storage containers and bedding, we can also look for a padded seat cushion?"

"Good idea," I sighed, twisting my legs into a Boy Scout knot in an effort to straighten my spine.

A week earlier, in late November of 2017, Dave and I had flown into Auckland. Since we planned to be in New Zealand for several months, it made more sense to buy a van and later sell it, than it did to rent one. So, we allotted ourselves one week in the big city to find a vehicle.

Dave and I had done lots of research, and we knew we wanted a diesel engine, high-top van. On the heels of our two-month African excursion in Bucky, the tent-topped pick-up truck, we knew we didn't want something that would require setting up and packing down each day. That process was exhausting. Plus, being in New Zealand, we needed a vehicle that was completely waterproof since we would probably pass several rainy days inside it.

At that time, New Zealand had a huge caravan culture. Unfortunately, November was spring and the beginning of their high season. It was a seller's market, and the best vehicles, like vans, were scarfed up quickly. Dave and I soon discovered that competition was fierce, and pickings were slim.

We spent our first week in Auckland in a hostel, perusing websites dedicated to buying and selling vehicles. Those pages seemed geared to young tourists, meaning the cars and vans being advertised were relatively inexpensive and had very high mileage. Most vehicles were too small for us, hatchbacks with mattresses crammed in the back, and I felt sure they had been driven hard, passed from one invincible 22-year-old to the next.

By our fifth day in the city, we were getting anxious and decided to brave used car dealerships. Eventually, in one of those lots, we found our van, a white Mitsubishi L300. I wish I could say we haggled ourselves a screaming deal. At best, we managed to get gently twisted instead of completely screwed.

The dealership specialized in quick, cheap campervan conversions. An old glass business work-van was transformed to become our campervan. It included a plywood bed with mattress pads, cheap carpet, slapped-together curtains, and a small sink at the back, which drained into plastic tubs. It was a petrol engine and a low top, but at least we could fully sit up in bed. It would do, and we were eager to get on the road.

With tiny skulls for door locks and a few gentle scrapes and dents, it was clear our van, like us, had history. Its front fender stuck out like an underbite, making our new digs resemble a bulldog. He needed a name, something tough and gritty. We settled on "Halen," in a nod to the band Van Halen.

It was time. We figured that we "might as well jump, go ahead and jump," so we hit the road.

Growing up, my big sister Julie had two friends who lived around the corner: Courtney and Brittany. Courtney and Brittany were sisters. Courtney was the oldest, and she was a very beautiful girl. However, the little sister Brittany was a showstopper, a strikingly gorgeous girl who could have been a model.

My well-meaning mother, who was always eager to establish an underdog and then root for the poor thing, felt bad for Courtney. It sounds very sweet in principle, but Mom sometimes had pity for those who weren't feeling disadvantaged. It would have been a bit like driving past a badass, overweight jogger and rolling down the window to shout, "Good job, Fluffy! I believe in you!" In a similar way, Mom had sincere compassion for poor Courtney.

"It just isn't fair that such a pretty girl becomes plain next to her sister," Mom explained to Julie and me.

For the first time at age eight, I came to notice that Courtney's eyes were a bit too widely spaced and that her curly hair edged toward frizzy on rainy days. From that day forward, Courtney grew more troll-like in my eyes. Bless her heart. In time, both sisters ended up pregnant by age 16, so I guess they got equal bang for their buck. I'm sure both girls became loving, fulfilled mothers, women who wouldn't have changed a thing. In fact, it was almost as if Courtney never realized she was disfigured. Nonetheless, I understood the gist of my mom's observation.

The islands of New Zealand were like Courtney and Brittany. The North Island was a beautiful place with beaches, vineyards, rolling hills, thermal features, and *three* volcanoes. Yet, compared to the South Island, with its snow-capped mountains, crystalline blue fjords, ancient creaking glaciers, thundering rivers, and all that wildlife to boot, the North paled in contrast.

Because Dave and I started our trip in New Zealand on the North Island, we didn't realize that its incredible beauty was relatively modest when compared to what lay ahead. Completely charmed, we explored the north for five weeks. She gave us plenty of bang for our buck along the way.

It wasn't long before we caught up with Gwen for our first Great Walk on the North Island. Three-and-a-half months had passed since we'd last seen Dave's sister, when we'd parted ways after our month together traveling through South Africa, Lesotho, and Kenya.

Great Walk 1 - Lake Waikaremoana

"Be welcomed into the homeland of the Tūhoe people. Trace the shoreline of Lake Waikaremoana, the 'sea of rippling waters,' through giant podocarp rainforest, remote beaches, and rugged mountains with stunning views."

We took three days and two nights to complete the level, 46-kilometer (29-mile) trail. By combining Days Two and Three to hike nine hours, we cut one night from the recommended itinerary. The weather was mostly fine, with a few late showers.

At the end of Day One, as we breathlessly reached the top of a steep climb, Dave, Gwen, and I approached our first-ever hut in New Zealand, the Panekire Hut. Half a dozen hikers sat, scattered on the wooden desk of a large, three-room bunkhouse. Their hiking boots and poles hung on hooks mounted to the outside walls. A corrugated tin roof pinged with gentle drizzle.

"How ya going? You made it," one woman greeted us.

Several others smiled in welcome. We made pleasantries about the hike and the weather as we offloaded our packs with relieved groans and freed our sweaty feet. Signs instructed us to leave our boots outside, so we did, and headed inside to explore.

Inside the wooden hut was a large common room with several tables, benches, and a wood-burning stove. On closer inspection we discovered a basic kitchen with two pump-water sinks and a couple of long countertops for food preparation. Attached to the common area were two identical rooms, each with long rows of adjacent bunk beds. The mattresses touched, meaning that nine little monkeys were meant to sleep side-by-side on top and the same would go on bottom, as well as in the other bunkroom. It was certainly cozy—a little too cozy for strangers.

The three of us chose bunks along the bottom, figuring it would make trips to the 'drop-toilets' out back a little easier at night. In time I would come to learn that the bottom bunks were coveted spots, and we were lucky to get them since the beds were first come, first serve. I spread out my sleeping bag next to Dave's. Because he lightly snores at night, I put myself on elbow duty so he wouldn't disturb the others.

We situated our belongings. I took off and hung my damp socks, and slipped on some flip-flops. (Later, I'd learn and love that the Kiwis called them "jandals" for 'Japanese sandals.') Back in the main room, one of the women was lighting a fire. We made our way to a table and claimed our space for the evening.

One of my favorite parts about traveling with Gwen was that she talked to people. On our own, Dave and I were more reserved. We tended to watch a room, with my face probably resting in its natural scowl. I was often too shy, too tired, or too deep in thought to successfully fake a smile. Gwen, however, had an inquisitive, approachable nature, and people felt comfortable around her. Like being in a peloton for human connection, I loved drafting on Gwen's likability. That night she helped us to get to know our hut-mates.

I'd read online that tourists accounted for more than 60 percent of all Great Walkers. That night, as we got to know our fellow hikers, we discovered that they were a diverse bunch. There were several languages being spoken around the hut. We met a German couple on their honeymoon and two young Swiss women. The Swiss girls had only just met. They were an interesting pair because one was German-speaking and the other was French-speaking, so English was our common language. Also, we met three sisters in their 60s from New Zealand with one's British boyfriend and a Kiwi mother and daughter who were celebrating the girl's high school graduation by hiking together. It was a fascinating collection of outdoorspeople.

Later, Dave, Gwen, and I made a meal of tuna, powdered milk, and cheesy noodles. After dinner, we played cards all evening with the Swiss girls. We headed to bed early, exhausted after a long day.

That night, I hadn't yet learned to bring earplugs. We were lucky that the people in our room were relatively quiet sleepers. Dave and Gwen seemed to rest well. However, I spent several hours awake, preoccupied with one man, the mature British boyfriend.

In the middle of the night, snorting and coughing woke me. It was the British boyfriend, above me, gagging on his own tongue. Alarmed, I listened closely. Every few minutes he just stopped breathing. I waited for agonizing seconds, quietly holding my breath as he held his. Between inhalations, I sometimes counted for up to a minute, beginning to wonder if he had died. Then, suddenly, he'd take an enormous gasping breath, sucking the life and his soul back into his body.

As my sleepless night wore on, I listened to the man fight for air, and a battle began to wage inside me, too. Equal parts of me worried over and wished for his death. I wondered if it would be best for everyone if I just slipped my camping pillow over his face and gently, *but firmly*, ended the misery.

That first night in Panekire Hut was a good introduction to all Great Walk hiking huts. We came to realize that on most Great Walks, the hikers could tramp in either direction. This meant half of the people in our hut had come from where we were next headed. They had trail experience to offer on what lay ahead. It also meant that the other half of our companions would be with us for several nights in a row. Over time, we would learn that this was great, if we enjoyed their company. It gave us an opportunity to meet and share multi-day hiking experiences with lovely folks from all over the world.

However, being in huts for multiple days with the same people could be challenging if they wore us out. For example, I would grow to dread the loud, self-advertising travelers in their 20s, those in constant competitions over who had been to the most places or had done the coolest things. We also tolerated back-talking children with their long-suffering parents, people who washed their feet in the sink, and large groups who set early morning alarms, waking the entire bunkroom with their crinkly packs and stage-whispers. Worst of all were the snorers who could rob an entire roomful of three to four nights' sleep because we were all headed in the same direction.

Overall, on the Lake Waikaremoana tramp and the eight Great Walks that followed, our positive interactions far outweighed the negative. Several of our connections started with handshakes and ended with an exchange of emails and even hugs. However, the deep desire to throttle one's hut-mates was also an integral part of any New Zealand tramping experience. It was all part of the plan. The Kiwis designed The Great Walks to be that way.

After our hike, we parted ways with Gwen. Her husband John was arriving from England, and they had their own exploring to do. We'd made plans to meet back up in a few weeks, on the South Island for Christmas. In the meantime, Dave and I would continue to explore the north.

As we crisscrossed the North Island, we began to fall in love with New Zealand's wide-open spaces and small-town feel. While the United Kingdom and New Zealand were roughly the same size, at that time, the former had a population of 66 million while the Kiwis only numbered 5 million. Kind and curious, folks made us feel welcome. Plus, given our history of living abroad in challenging places, we relished in New Zealand's developed ease, and it was refreshing to speak the local language for once.

As a backdrop to the lovely people, New Zealand offered vineyards with wine tastings, creative craft beers, divine chocolates, and gourmet ice cream. The coffee was fantastic, even at gas stations, where the cashiers doubled as baristas. Small businesses thrived, with Ma and Pa shops on every corner. Signs advertising "Art" stood outside of random homes down country lanes. The fish and chips were world-class, and the sun was plentiful, albeit strange. It seared our flesh in direct light, yet we needed another layer if we moved to the shade, giving me the perfect excuse to buy more gear! To top it off, the wilderness was accessible and curiously safe, with no snakes or scorpions or lions or bears. At every stop, volcanoes, mountains, beaches, rivers, or lakes beckoned us to come outside and play.

Basically, Dave and I had found our paradise.

Great Walk 2 - Tongariro Northern Circuit

"From alpine herb fields to forests, from tranquil lakes to desert plateaux, journey through a landscape of stark contrasts with amazing views in this World Heritage site. Winding past Mount Tongariro and Mount Ngauruhoe, you will be dazzled by dramatic volcanic landscapes and New Zealand's rich geological and ancestral past."

We took three days and two nights to complete the level 43-km (27-m) trail, doubling down the last day to skip the final hut. We had sunny, fine weather for the entire walk.

I had a girl crush on Sunny, our hut ranger the first night. At 24, she was lean, athletic, mixed-race Māori/white, and working for the National Parks. She was just so natural and confident and cool.

During the evening introduction and safety briefing, Sunny commanded the attention of our hut-mates, most of whom were high school students on their Duke of Edinburgh Gold Challenge (an intensive, comprehensive, outdoor challenge for teens). Sunny spoke in both English and Te Reo, the beautiful Māori language, to give her talk. Those who weren't already in love with her just went on ahead and fell. The entire room ate from Sunny's hand.

In terms of practical safety, Sunny pointed out the fire exits and taught us how to turn off the gas cookers. In the event of a volcanic eruption, however, Sunny had less to offer. She hoped that we were good runners, and suggested we "sprint like hell to higher ground." Sunny said that one of the volcanoes was long overdue for an eruption so we should, you know, "just be aware." Her crack was funny at the time. Little did we all know that another volcano would erupt in New Zealand, almost two years later, killing five people.

Sunny went on to explain that the volcanoes were sacred places to the Māori people, and she asked that we *not* undertake the two-hour 'optional side-trip' to summit Mount Ngauruhoe. Most tourists, like myself, were huge *Lord of the Rings* fans, and the opportunity to hike to the top of "Mount Doom" from Peter Jackson's films was a tempting detour. However, doing so had led to several injuries, damaged the landscape, and upset the native people. The government was working to educate tourists, and Sunny encouraged us to spread the word.

She closed by wishing us well on the rest of our hike and on our travels throughout New Zealand. Sunny reminded us that, "We (the Māori) don't feel that we own this land, but we were put here to take care of it."

Because it was early December and the last week of the school year, we saw several school groups on the second day of the circuit, on a portion that could be completed as an alpine day hike. Classic adolescent dramas played out before our eyes; a distraught computer geek hyperventilated on her first-ever serious hike, while, up ahead, an impatient, future divorce lawyer over-took two band nerds, shoving them from her path when the teacher's head was turned. Most were awkward, boisterous, sweaty 13-year-olds, crisping in splotches from poorly applied sunscreen.

At one point, Dave shouted at some boys who were throwing rocks over our heads into the sulfuric lake he was trying to photograph. Later, we all gathered to watch a helicopter land to pick up "Caitlyn's Mom," a parent chaperone who had twisted her ankle. It was a cruel fate for poor Caitlyn, who had undoubtedly begged her mother to keep a low profile. It was also rough for us, two teachers on a year's sabbatical. We loved kids, truly, but we deserved a break from the smelly goblins.

Beneath the gaze of the two fiery gods, we trudged up dusty rust-col-ored hills and down volcanic moonscapes of rock and shale. We wove through a panorama of smoking emerald ponds, an enormous red gashed crater, and a sapphire blue lake. Young and old, we journeyed together, encouraging each other to finish the quest.

Our second Great Walk, The Tongariro Northern Circuit, was an epic voyage through middle earth and middle school.

Great Walk 3 - Whanganui Journey

"Experience the beauty, history and cultural significance of the winding Whanganui River...featuring the most scenic stretches of the river through remote hills and valleys."

We took three days and two nights to complete the 87-km (54-m) river journey. On the only boating trip of the Great Walks, we had mostly sunny weather with a few pockets of showers.

Two calves walked through the front door of the house and milled around the entryway.

"Uhm, Jonno," Dave interrupted our lecturer a few moments later. "... Look behind you."

Our 20-year-old canoe instructor Jonno paused at the whiteboard, a dried-out marker poised over a faint, unclear sketch. He turned to look over his shoulder.

"Oh Christ! Muuuum!" Jonno yelled into the kitchen. "Sorry about this, guys," he said, turning back to Dave, me, and the other 10 canoeing students.

"Mum! Come get these cows before they shit all over the house again!" He cringed slightly, remembering his audience.

"I'm making the coffees!" his mother bellowed back. "Can you take care of it?"

"Geeze, Mum! It's not like I'm busy here," Jonno huffed. "Sorry about this. Excuse me just a minute."

Both Jonno and his mother rushed from opposite ends of the house into the foyer, and together they herded the calves out the front door. In addition to having a homestay, campground, and canoe rental, it seemed that Jonno and his family raised farm animals. We would later learn that the babies were ready for their bottle feeding.

Our classmates that morning, like us, were new to boating. In fact, by a show of hands, Dave and I were the most experienced in the group, having had five days of whitewater kayaking lessons a couple of months earlier in the year. These boats weren't kayaks, but rather large, more buoyant, two-person Canadian canoes with space for dry barrels to hold our personal belongings and snacks. There would be no instructor or guide with us on the trip, so our five days of practice 'reading' river water might help. As we figured it, the trip was one of the Great Walks, an outing designed for idiot tourists, so how hard could it be? Worst-case scenario, we were both very strong swimmers.

(Little did we know that thick black freshwater eels, the size of human legs, also swam in those waters.)

Cows situated, Jonno returned to our lesson.

"Look where you want to go, *not* where you *don't* want to go. So, if you're headed toward a rock, don't look at it! But, if you can't help it, and you're definitely going to hit the rock, then lean into it, not away from it, and you'll be sweet as."

'Sweet as' was a Kiwi expression that Dave and I had grown to love. Similar to American 'awesome' or British 'brilliant,' this versatile hanging simile allowed one's mind to fill in the blank. Sweet as what? Something super sweet, no doubt.

The 20-minute lesson included a toy boat segment with stones from the garden. Jonno made skid and crashing sounds, 'Eeeeerrk, prrrrkkhh,' as he highlighted potential obstacles we might encounter. After that, we watched a video of the river journey in fast forward, which previewed each of the rapids for us. The briskly changing scenes flashed across the screen, into my mind, and right back out again.

"Basically, if you forget everything I've said, just go left the first two days and right on the last day," Jonno summarized.

No problem.

When we got to the put-in, Dave and I decided it would be best if he rode in the back. Based on our limited kayaking experience, I begrudgingly admitted that he had better boat control and a more natural sense of how to use the paddle to steer. We loaded up and launched into the river without any issues. It was a gentle current with plenty of time to find our rhythm.

As we worked our way downstream, I began to better understand my role in the arrangement. Essentially, my job up front was to toil incessantly like a whipping boy. I was to shut up, paddle, and leave the long-term planning and creative solutions to Dave.

My career had prepared me well for this role, but I still struggled to let Dave have complete control. I felt certain that our third 'Great Walk,' the Whanganui Journey, had been responsible for more than one divorce. Wisely, they left that part off the website.

Three days would come to feel like 30.

"Are you even paddling?" I shouted occasionally over my aching shoulders.

"Yeees, Madam," Dave would sigh.

He sounded incredibly relaxed back there.

As the river miles added up, we found our groove. We had a few exciting moments on the way, but nothing we didn't manage. Any 'fear' we experienced as we approached and then ran the rapids was more fun than scary. Most of the time the river was calm, and the nature was restorative. As novice boaters, we enjoyed ourselves.

My favorite Māori cultural experience took place on the Whanganui Journey.

After a full day of paddling, on our second afternoon, we began to see signs for our evening hut, "Tieke Kainga," coming up on river left. Both Jonno and the brochures had prepared us for our stay. This hut would be special. Adjacent to a traditional Māori sacred house, known as a "marae," our second hut would be run by volunteer Māori community members.

On the shore, we took special care to carry our canoe high up the slope of the beach, and to tie it tightly to a tree. We had been warned that the river could rise several feet overnight. Evidently, it wasn't uncommon for unthinking tourists to have their boats swept downstream as they slept. *Oops.*

Once the canoe was secured, we lugged our life vests, helmets, and the first load of dry barrels up a sandy hill to the hut. It would take a couple more arduous trips to get all our gear to the top. There a Māori woman met us.

"Kia Ora! Welcome to Tieke Kainga. Please come in," she greeted us warmly.

She introduced herself as Aroha and showed us into the hut. It seemed like hosting might be new to Aroha because she was very detailed in her tour. It was clear she wanted to do a good job, which I respected. I guessed her to be about Dave's age, in her mid-50s.

Actually, at the top of the hill there were two buildings. Our hut with its kitchen, bunkhouse, and deck sat to the right. Aroha welcomed us into this space. On the left, however, was the marae, the meetinghouse. It was a small, white, understated structure, yet intricate carvings framed the house's roof and doorway. In front of the house, on a large green lawn, stood an enormous red wooden pole. Fantastic faces of people and animals were carved into the pole. It was clearly of cultural significance, and it almost seemed to protect the space.

"Please get settled and rest. I'll just ask that you not step on the lawn yet, not until I've had a chance to talk to your whole group. We have something special planned once everyone arrives," Aroha explained.

Dave and I finished hauling our gear up from the boat, chose bunks, changed shoes, and relaxed on the deck with a cup of tea and a snack. As we waited for the others to arrive, I felt a little apprehensive. We had read that there would be a Māori ceremony and that we would be asked to participate. I dreaded the possibility that I might be asked to speak or perform somehow. After all, I was a shy woman who could get worked up and weird when she had to order pizza over the phone.

Eventually, our hut-mates trickled in and situated themselves. There were two young German women in their early 20s. Also, a young married couple and her mother joined us from England.

Once we were ready and gathered on the desk, Aroha explained the "pōwhiri," or welcoming ceremony. We quickly ran through the format with Aroha, and then she walked us around to the entrance at the top of the lawn. It was time to get started.

The pōwhiri began with Aroha's husband Niko standing in front of the meetinghouse. He spoke a few words in Te Reo, holding a staff as he paced and talked in a strong, almost aggressive way. He paused and Aroha sang a song of welcome and motioned us forward to sit on benches.

Once we were seated, Niko continued with his speech, still in Te Reo. While I couldn't understand his words, his body language was slightly intimidating. Gradually, I realized that we were being welcomed, but it was a warrior's welcome. Similar to the rugby "haka," which evolved from a traditional Māori war dance, Niko's message also seemed fierce, but it was somehow friendlier. Then Aroha sang another song.

Before the ritual, Aroha had explained to us that in Māori tradition, women were not allowed to speak at these ceremonies. Men spoke to protect their families from danger. Instead of talking, women sang to honor their husbands and thank them for their protection. Therefore, for the next step in the service, the men among us would make our introductions.

It didn't sit well with any of us that the women were not supposed to speak. However, Dave and I recognized that we were there to learn about another culture, not to enforce our own. Dave stood to introduce me, as well as the two German women, since they had no man to represent them. After that, the British son-in-law stood and introduced his wife and mother-in-law. The British women sang "All Things Bright and Beautiful," a children's church hymn in England. It was silly and sweet, and we all giggled a bit in awkwardness. I appreciated them having the courage to step up.

Formalities finished, we approached our hosts. Aroha welcomed each of the women with a "hongi," a ceremonial touching of noses. Niko did the same with the men. Officially welcomed, we were in!

Aroha then gave us a brief tour to describe the cultural significance of the meetinghouse. First, Aroha explained that the pouwhenua (post) was carved with the faces of ancestors, and it was meant to protect travelers on the river. She also told of the significance of the fern leaf, saying that its reflective underside illuminated paths at night, guiding the Māori home. Finally, Aroha enlightened us on the significance of the Whanganui River to her people.

"The river is sacred. Most tourists on this trip don't want to fall into the water. I understand. However, if you do fall in, just remember, it's actually a blessing!"

After our experience at Tieke Kainga, thanks to Aroha, Niko, and their community, I felt less like a tourist in New Zealand. They'd shared their culture and warm hospitality. As a result, I felt a deeper connection and even more respect for the country, like a guest welcomed into someone's home.

For our final day of the Whanganui Journey, Jonno had warned us about the penultimate feature, the 'Fifty-Fifty Rapid.' It was the most exciting rapid of the trip. Evidently, those were our chances of surviving it without swimming: 50/50.

That last day, late in the afternoon as we rounded a bend, we were surprised to see several boats and teenage boys scattered across the river up ahead. It was a tableau of catastrophe! However, the boys were clearly having a fantastic time.

In front of us, one canoe rode very low in the water, holding five boys who had squeezed into two seats. They were headed toward an enormous rapid, which could only be the Fifty-Fifty. Downstream, two other capsized boats were partially submerged. Flailing swimmers pulled the crafts to shore. Also, several very wet paddlers struggled on the rocky beach, draining their waterlogged boats. Meanwhile, another set of boys was portaging their boat upriver, heading back upstream to do it all over again.

It was a lot to take in. As Dave and I absorbed the scene, we suddenly realized how quickly we were gaining speed. It was too late to pull over to plan our execution. We were being sucked in. And fast! There was only one good option.

"Shall we go for it?" Dave shouted from behind me.

I swallowed the lack of choice and steeled myself.

"Okay. Let's do it!"

So we lined ourselves up, centered on the meat of the Fifty-Fifty Rapid, and paddled full speed ahead.

Of course, our odds weren't good. We were faced with the "50-50-90 Rule," a theory developed by the late American humorist Andy Rooney: *Anytime you have a 50-50 chance of getting something right, there's a 90 percent probability you'll get it wrong.*

As we crested the first wave of the rapid, a wall of water met us on the other side. It crashed over the front of the boat, swamping the inside. I was almost completely dunked but just managed to keep my head above water. Later, in a spectacular photo that a very nice man on the shore took of us, we would see that Dave had been completely submerged while still sitting in the back of our boat. In the blink of an eye, the canoe tilted right, and we both spilled out.

The current was swift and shockingly chilly, but more exciting than frightening. With a great deal of effort, we managed to swim the paddles, the boat, and ourselves over to the side of the river. Thankfully, we'd remembered to tie down the barrels inside, which held our belongings, but it made the canoe extremely heavy. On the shore, we slumped, exhausted, onto the sand. We lay flat on our backs and panted for several minutes.

"You all right?" Dave asked, after he caught his breath.

I looked at him and smiled.

"I'm great," I laughed.

After all, the Whanganui River had blessed us.

As the first month passed, we settled in and added several improvements to Van Halen. Dave rigged up a system of bungee cords to hold several storage containers in place. We had a coat rack, solar-powered twinkle lights, a charging system for our electronics, and even a console to hold our cups, something he'd cleverly crafted from a Pepsi Max carton. Our two biggest additional purchases were a rooftop storage box and a top-of-the-line chilly bin (ice cooler). For 250 NZD, it kept items cold for almost five days, as it *bloody well* should have for that price. I even managed to level the front seat for me with patio chair cushions, making all those hours on twisty roads more comfortable. An ongoing project for Dave's innovative mind, the van evolved continuously.

Our van was certified "Self-Contained," meaning that, technically, we had all that was required for us to "freedom camp" in designated, *free*, highly-sought-after parking locations. However, these spots were difficult to find and claim because so many others wanted them too. To qualify for the permit, the van held two fresh water tanks, a sink, a grey wastewater tank, and a trash can with its requisite lid. We also had the compulsory toilet, which was a plastic cube with a seat on top, the size of a cat's litter box. However, we never once used it, tossing it into the roof box. Instead, we stopped at one of the (clearly-marked, numerous) public restrooms or cafés.

To me, it seemed that the self-contained, freedom camping option was more intended for fully loaded RVs, but we, like countless others, squeaked by with the bare legal minimum. New Zealand's tourist infrastructure was fantastic, but it was becoming overburdened. Irresponsible freedom campers were a growing problem for the country. There were too many tourists shitting in alleyways and dumping their trash behind bushes.

Over the five months, Dave and I would end up freedom-camping only a handful of times. We quickly realized that we preferred campgrounds. Most nights we paid less than 20 NZD per person for access to hot showers, flush toilets, a full kitchen, and Internet. Plus, we were guaranteed a spot, so we did not spend hours of our limited time looking for places to park. Consequently, for a little extra expense, our basic van life in New Zealand was easy and comfortable.

Those first five weeks on the North Island passed quickly, but we covered a lot of ground. From the northernmost lighthouse on Cape Reinga to the windy, southern shores of Wellington we'd done most of it, if not *all*. In addition to the three North Island Great Walks, we passed through several major cities—Auckland, Taupo, Napier, and Wellington. We dug our own spa at a hot water beach in the Coromandel and waded through a thermal stream in Rotarua. We scratched our nerd itch at Peter Jackson's Hobbiton and found Golem and other special effects at the Weta Workshop. But before we knew it, it was time to catch the ferry and cross to the South Island.

The South Island

Great Walk 4 - Heaphy Track

"If it's varied and rugged landscapes with mountain views you're looking for, you'll be spoilt for choice on the Heaphy Track. Travel through expansive tussock downs, lush forests and nīkau palms to the roaring seas of the West Coast."

We took four days and three nights to complete the longest Great Walk, a 78-km (48-m) tramp. We had fine, sunny weather all four days.

"Madam, can you help me, please? My bra is twisted again," Dave groaned.

"Hold still a minute. Man, this side is worse," I sighed, and straightened him out.

Dave's camera bra was a constant issue. A wonderful photographer, Dave had designed a system for quick camera access while hiking. He wore the camera centered on his chest, clipped to his backpack shoulder straps with a couple of carabiners. However, it often got flipped around, and the whole set-up seemed uncomfortable, too. He couldn't wait to fling that thing off at the end of a long day.

We knew our gear well by the time Dave and I started the Heaphy Track, our fourth Great Walk. We had the organization of our meals, sleeping bags, clothing, and other essentials streamlined. I knew exactly which pocket of my backpack held the spork, and I could locate my headlamp in the dark. But as the Kiwis said, "it all went to custard" if I didn't put my things back exactly where they belonged. And of course, whatever I needed was inevitably at the bottom of my pack.

Over the years, we'd developed a hiking hack—to bring alternate pairs of quick drying socks and underwear, as well as some safety pins and a tiny container of soap. Each night we could give dirty laundry a quick rinse, and those items could dry the next day while pinned to the outside of our packs. In theory it was a wonderful routine, but in reality we changed once or twice in the middle of the tramp. Then, we stuffed our salty, snail-skidded laundry somewhere deep and dark in our backpacks.

Many Kiwis stayed ahead of the grime by changing into their "togs" (swimsuits) at the end of a long hiking day. They went in search of the nearest arctic swimming hole for a refreshing icy dip. However, a true child of Texas, I loathed being cold for long, and I was usually too tired for a second outing anyway. Dave and I spent our tramps in New Zealand marinating in our own funk. By the end of the Heaphy, and every other Great Walk, I was desperate for a long, hot shower.

Speaking of snail skids, the Heaphy Track was known for its 'Giant Carnivorous' snails. With shells that could grow to the size of scones, these gastropods survived mostly on earthworms. One hut ranger told us to keep our eyes peeled. If we were lucky, she said, we might see a snail slurping up an earthworm like spaghetti. I was sorry we didn't.

The track was also where we first encountered the South Island's two main bugs: bumblebees and sand flies. The bumblebees were almost cute— slow, fat, fuzzy characters from children's books. Surprisingly, they were drawn to the color blue, which accounted for 82 percent of my wardrobe. I spent too much time in frozen terror, swarmed by bees. Ultimately, their attention convinced me to buy a different-colored hiking shirt, which helped.

The notorious West Coast sand flies were an even bigger problem. Horrible creatures, these little biting bastards found any inch of skin left unsprayed or uncovered. I commonly felt the first nips on my ankles, or worse, on my knuckles. We would come to battle these ruthless critters for months.

Overall, the Heaphy Track was long and relatively gentle. Each of the four days felt like a different level in a video game as the backdrop shifted in stages. A mountain bike trail at some times of year, the path was generally smooth, wide, and mostly level. My temperamental knees loved the terrain.

After we finished the Heaphy walk, we raced east across the country to meet up with Gwen's family for Christmas in Christchurch.

Christmas in Christchurch

One of the best parts about marrying Dave was inheriting Gwen and her family, and it was pure serendipity that six of us were able to meet up in New Zealand. Primarily a collection of educators, we were all taking a break from our careers in one way or another. Be it a short holiday, a sabbatical, or possibly retirement, we were catching our breaths, reevaluating our professions, and contemplating if and how things should change in the future. It was an extraordinary life pause for each of us, one that bizarrely overlapped at the bottom of the world for Christmas.

Gwen's husband John, a university lecturer on winter break, had come down from England to join her a month earlier. The two had made the North and South Island rounds together. Their daughter Penelope (Penny) and her husband Jeffrey, 28-year-olds, were taking a year off to travel before starting a family. They had been in the country since November but planned to explore until February. Dave and I were on the gap year and seven weeks into our five months in New Zealand. We were only missing Penny's younger brother Derek and Dave's daughter Paige, who were on their own paths elsewhere in the world.

The family hired a house in Christchurch for Christmas week and filled it with food, curiosity, puzzles, reasoned speculation, and laughter.

It felt strange to have Christmas in summer. During that time we explored the area, taking little day walks in t-shirts on the hills above town. We got too warm hiking on the Banks Peninsula, too. In the sunny garden, we napped, barbequed, drank Pimms and played Kubb, a lawn game with wooden blocks. On a balmy Christmas Evening in 2017, we attended the "70th Annual YMCA Carols by Candlelight," a sing-along in downtown Christchurch. Best of all, on Christmas Day, my British family and I put on our "swimming costumes" and headed to Sumner Beach to take a Yuletide dip in the ocean. I loved that "swimming costumes" made it sound as if I'd dressed up as a freckled, 41-year-old Christmas beachcomber, rather than just being one.

Too soon, our week together came to an end. Poor John, the only person with a job, returned to England to work. Dave and I were thrilled to have Gwen and the youngsters join us on our fifth Great Walk, the Abel Tasman Track.

Great Walk 5 - Abel Tasman

"Blessed with a mild climate, golden beaches, and lush coastal native bush, the Abel Tasman Coast Track has it all. Choose to hike the whole track, water taxi between different locations, or kayak from Marahau to campsites in the southern section of the track at any time of the year."

We planned for five days and four nights to complete this 60-km (37-m) beachside tramp. With showers forecasted on four of the five days, we wore our raingear, lined our packs with trash sacks, put on their rain covers, and crossed our fingers.

Of all the Great Walks, the Abel Tasman was arguably the easiest. With huts near beaches and water taxis, it was certainly the most accessible to the general public. Jet boats could drop a person near each of the huts. For a fee, it was possible to have your bags delivered, enabling you to hike with just a daypack. Others chose to sea kayak in the bays or spend a day on the beach, taking a water taxi back to their car in the late afternoon. However, our family stuck with the Great Walk program, and we were loaded down with gear for a full five days of tramping.

Tidal crossings were a unique challenge on this hike. For most crossings, there were direct, low-tide routes, but if your timing was off, slightly longer alternative high-tide paths were available. There was only one tidal crossing on Day Three, the Awaroa Inlet, with no alternative option, so hikers were required to cross within two hours either side of low tide. Depending on the cycle and a person's luck, that window might start at noon, or worse, at four o'clock in the morning. However, the hut rangers did an excellent job of keeping guests informed. Building up to the big event, I felt a little uneasy; however, I would end up with other things to worry about.

On that first day of the hike, walking with Jeffrey and Penny was like racing people on the conveyor belts at the airport while remaining on the firm ground. Jeff was a professional contemporary dancer, and the two of them glided along at roughly at one-and-one-third the speed of average human beings. However, the conversation was good, so I held pace with them for most of that beachy, forested day. If my joints were smoking, I didn't notice.

Later, about 30 minutes from the day's end at the Anchorage Hut, I snagged suddenly, in pain. In three steps, my left knee went from feeling perfectly fine to being barely able to manage a step. I downplayed it to my British nephew.

"Wait a second. Hold on. I think I've done something," I said to Jeff.

I swore loud and long inside my head.

The pain I felt was not the chronic pain I had grown used to. At the recommendation of a sports medicine doctor, I'd given up running and contact sports by age 35 because I'd already burned through too much of my cartilage. He suggested I save what remained of my knees for other activities, like hiking. Contributing to the problem, I suspected that my joints were actually made of peppermint candy rather than bone, cracking off and snapping off into bite size little chunks. I'd learned to suck on, to suck up that kind of pain. This injury was sharper, making me wince with each downhill step. This new sensation—this was lightning lemon pain.

Since we were very near the hut, I encouraged the others to go ahead. I loaded up on painkillers, and lemon-gingerly hobbled the final 30 minutes to our next hut. That evening, I took it very easy and hoped I would miraculously heal overnight.

In the Anchorage Hut, a full cast of characters entertained our family that evening. Most of them were Kiwis on summer holiday, celebrating the first week of the New Year. It was a great sampling of locals and a good reminder that there are all types in all cultures. Our favorite Kiwi on the Abel Tasman Track was a woman we called "Negligee Nancy."

Secretly, I envied Negligee Nancy. She was one of those humans who either didn't know or *truly* didn't care what those around her were thinking. Fantastically oblivious, Nancy played her radio at full volume on the hut deck, shouted at other people's children, and elbowed her way into the kitchen space, cutting in front of those who waited in line. She inserted herself into any conversation that she reckoned would benefit from her input, and she even invited herself to join one stammering couple, also Kiwis, the following day. Best of all, throughout the evening, she wore a silky, teeny-tiny nightgown over her braless, very average, late-30s figure.

The woman had more body confidence and just plain confidence-confidence than I'd ever known. Too prudish, too sensitive, and too self-conscious, a part of me wanted to *be* Nancy. She was delightfully scandalous, and I probably needed a dash more of what she had. For better or worse, Negligee Nancy owned her world.

The next day Nancy's alarm got the entire bunkhouse off to a nice early start. She and the couple she commandeered hit the trail, and our family had a groggy, leisurely breakfast. An hour later, we began our walk for the day.

The morning hiking started off well. I ate two anticipatory Ibuprofens, and I was able to walk for about an hour. Unfortunately, it wasn't long before I felt that sinister snag again, and walking downhill became almost impossible. The family was lovely about it, but I felt embarrassed, as if I'd become the American diva that British stoics expected me to be.

I asked myself, "WWNND?" What Would Negligee Nancy Do? I quickly realized there was no way she would have finished the hike on a knee like mine. Nancy would have asked the family to fashion a makeshift litter and to carry her back to the Anchorage Hut. However, I figured I could make it slowly, on my own legs, so Dave and I decided to turn back.

I took another four painkillers, and ol' steadfast Sir walked me back to the first hut. The others would continue as planned. Mercifully, it being the Abel Tasman, I was able to catch a water taxi back to the beginning of the hike. Of all the Great Walks to have had an injury, this was the best one because there was an easy option out. In that way, I was very lucky.

Later that afternoon, I was able to get an appointment with a doctor in the nearest town. Her diagnosis was "femoral patella syndrome," an overuse injury, given all the hiking I'd done in the past year. She also said blithely to load up on painkillers because, at 41, I wasn't getting any younger. I'm not a whiner or a drama queen, and I resented her suggestion that I hadn't just muscled through the pain.

Mind you, at least 15 years older than me, the doctor was no spring chicken herself. My scrappy ego was insulted that she'd prematurely aged me, too. I felt pretty sure that Negligee Nancy would have tackled the quack. Inside me, sweet Astrid thought a rumble sounded 'sweet as.' I took a calming breath. Instead, like the mature woman I was becoming, whether I liked it or not, I just fake-smiled and thanked Dr. Fart Breath for her time.

Here's the thing: the medical explanation didn't jibe with me because it only seemed to address ongoing chronic pain. To me, it didn't explain the new, acute pain that had kept me from finishing the hike. Still, the prognosis was positive, which was what I wanted to hear. I still had three more months in New Zealand, and four more Great Walks to complete.

That evening, we found a campsite near the trail and signed me up for three nights. The next morning, Dave caught a water taxi back to the first hut, doubled down, and met back up with the family for the final two nights of the walk. Meanwhile, alone, I holed up in the van to contemplate my failing body, growing older, and the inescapable death of all living things.

Three days later, I was happy when the family returned. They'd enjoyed the Abel Tasman Track and, mercifully, had better weather than forecasted. Of course, being sympathetic and discreet, they didn't rub my nose in it. My knee was doing better, but I was glad our next Great Walk wasn't for another three weeks. I would give it a nice long rest.

The five of us spent another couple of days together on the north coast in Nelson. This city became Dave's and my favorite in New Zealand and our "maybe one day" dream home in the world. That January, we rented bicycles from "The Lazy Cyclist" which was perfect for me and my knee. We rode along the Great Taste Trail, stopping at gourmet cafés and vineyards along the way to savor cheese, cakes, chocolate, coffee, and pinot. Life couldn't get any better.

Finally, it was time to say goodbye to Penny and Jeffrey, who were crossing to the North Island. We would miss their sparkle and fizz; those two made everything more fun. We also parted ways, just for a short time, with Gwen. She was eager to try some solo travel after she dropped her kids at the ferry terminal. It would be an emotional parting for them, a spectacular ending to a family chapter.

"Everyone! Could I have everyone's attention, please?" I announced to the empty van in my haughtiest Queen's English.

Back to being a meager family of two, Dave and I began to beef up our numbers.

"Let's take a vote. Raise your hand if you would like to stop for coffee," I polled.

I raised my hand. Dave didn't, mostly because he didn't drink coffee.

"Really, Sir? You're going to pressure everyone else in the family into doing what *you* want to do? That seems rather selfish," I teased.

"Let's vote again," I continued, "Put your hand up if you would like to stop for coffee."

Dave sighed. We both raised our hands.

"Fantastic!" I clapped twice in celebration. "I'm glad we could all reach an agreement."

For the next fortnight, we crisscrossed the South Island, high-fiving Gwen when our paths overlapped. While she struck out on her own, we tried freedom-camping again, washing our pits in the river and miserably holding it for 12 hours until a public toilet opened. During that time, we also ate lots of fish n' chips and chocolate-covered pineapple lumps. Each day, I took my neck-breaking afternoon nap as Dave drove along twisty country roads.

During those weeks, we also visited the Queen Charlotte Track, which was surprisingly not one of the Great Walks. Gwen did some of it alone, and Dave joined her for a later portion. Meanwhile, I drank tea in the van and shooed away cheeky wekas—troublesome, brown, nosey, kiwi-bird imposters. By this point in the trip, my knee and I had adopted a new personal policy against "extra walks." Plus, Brother and Sister liked to push themselves, and I was secretly relieved for a good excuse not to join the Terminator Siblings for a nine-hour jaunt in the rain.

Zigzagging across the country, we haphazardly made our way south. During this time, we took the first of two week-long whitewater kayaking courses in Murchison. Later, in Kaikura, we went on a whale watching cruise and spotted two great humpbacks and a pod of orca. On the West Coast, we visited the Fox and Franz Joseph glaciers and were shocked by photographs showing their rapid demise. We explored an old western-like Arrow town and fell in love with Wanaka, enjoying the shopping, the fantastic Patagonia ice cream, and the spectacular views of ski slopes in summer. Other than a visit to the Department of Conservation office for hiking information, we decided to give the touristy Queenstown a miss.

Each time we caught up with Gwen, her confidence as an independent traveler and hiker had grown. In passing, she regaled us with stories of hikes she'd completed, hitchhikers she had picked up, and of the one time as a hitchhiker that she'd been picked up by a base jumper—the ones who wore bat-suits and jumped off the sides of cliffs!

Eventually, the three of us met up at the bottom of the South Island and took a ferry to Rakiura, for the sixth Great Walk.

Great Walk 6 – Rakiura Track

"Escape on an island adventure and relax in peaceful surroundings with the bush, birds, and beach at your side. Follow this leisurely circuit track along open coastline, through forest and along Paterson Inlet's sheltered shores."

We took three days and two nights, to tramp this 32-km (19-m) forested trail. It was dry and sunny all three days.

Rakiura, or Steward Island, was the small island just below New Zealand's South Island. At the time, the island boasted about 400 permanent residents and was off the typical tourist track, so it was a quiet place. With Rakiura National Park making up more about 85 percent of Stewart Island, we had a unique opportunity to see native plants and birds in the wild and to learn about New Zealand's logging history. Most importantly to us, Stewart Island was said to offer the best chance of spotting the famous, nocturnal kiwi bird, for which New Zealanders were nicknamed.

After a three-week break from walking, I was both apprehensive and hopeful about how my knee would handle the hike. Superstar Dave took the brunt of our weight, carrying all of our food and daily water, so that I could lighten the load on my leg. The terrain was quite easy, and we took it slow. Thankfully, I was able to manage the tramp without any major issues.

As with all the Great Walks, each evening the hut rangers gave interesting talks on safety, history, wildlife, and the trails. My understanding of New Zealand deepened through those months, and on Rakiura, the magnitude of New Zealand's loss of birdlife was driven home to me.

I learned that humans, Polynesians, first settled New Zealand in 1250. Europeans did not arrive until 1642. Prior to that, other than a few species of bat and some marine mammals, the islands had *no* indigenous mammals. Zero land mammals. Instead, the islands were positively covered in birds. Moreover, one ranger told us that when Captain James Cook arrived in the

1770s, he wrote that the bird song was deafening. Cook said then men slept on the ship instead of the land, in order to get some rest.

Of course, with Man came trouble. First, the Māori brought dogs and rats. Later, bursting with bright ideas, the Europeans introduced rabbits, pigs, weasels, stoats, and a whole pack of other problems. Through a series of environmental chain reactions, the bird population was decimated. In fact, since humans first arrived up to the time of our trip in 2018, almost 50 percent of New Zealand's bird species, many of which were flightless, had gone extinct!

Part of me wished we'd been able to see the ostrich-like 'moa,' which were 12 feet tall (3 meters) and 500 lbs (225 kg). I tried to imagine its primary predator, the enormous 'Haast's eagle,' which was estimated to attack at speeds of 50 mph (80 kmph). Both of these beasties were still alive when the settlers first arrived! The aging, gimpy pragmatic in me wasn't too torn up over their disappearance when I imagined the blast of air, the gutting talons, and being swept fiercely into the sky.

Huge animal conservation efforts were in place all over New Zealand, and it was still possible to see all kinds of birds, including endangered ones, especially on the well-isolated Stewart Island. During our five months in New Zealand, I would learn to identify robins, riflemen, fantails, bellbirds, tomtits, kia, weka, and the blue duck. However, there was one famous bird we had trouble spotting.

"Shhhhh. Did you hear that?" Dave whispered.

Gwen and I froze and listened.

Nothing.

It was 9 p.m. and dark outside on our second night. We were in the woods near the North Arm Hut, slowly combing the trail with our red-light head torches.

We'd been told that kiwis made distinctive sounds. The male had a loud, shrill call, said to resemble its name, "keee-weee, keeee-weeee." The female was different. Earlier, the ranger had tried to replicate the sound, straining so much I worried he was going to burst something. The sound he produced was a grunty, gravelly rhythm, something like a prehistoric raptor who smoked.

The ranger told us that kiwis mated for life but that they often slept in separate burrows. When darkness fell, they woke and called each other, to check in. After living with Dave for months in a campervan, I thought the kiwis might be onto something. Outside in the darkness that night, we hoped to hear the couples' greetings.

"There! You hear that?" Dave hissed.

In the distance, we heard a male calling and stumbled our way in that direction. When we got closer, we stopped and waited quietly for a few minutes.

"Presumably, if we sit here for long enough, he might cross our path," Gwen speculated.

So we held still for about 10 minutes in the pitch black. Occasionally, small groups of our hut-mates would shuffle past, startling when they got close enough for our shapes to appear in their darkness.

"Did you guys see it?" one guy asked excitedly. "There was one outside the hut a few minutes ago!"

Bugger! We'd just missed it.

After another half hour, we decided to give up. It had been a long day hiking and we were ready to hit the sack. We used our flashlights to creep carefully back to the hut. Dave and I climbed into our bunks, while Gwen took care of her evening routine outside.

A few minutes later, she rushed back into the room.

"You guys! I just saw a kiwi!" she whispered excitedly. "Come on!"

We jumped back out of bed and followed her outside.

"I was coming out of the toilet, and it crossed the path, right over there."

Gwen's tone managed to turn her triumph into an apology. I hated that she felt the need to be sorry, but I appreciated her genuine disappointment on our behalf. Since she didn't gloat, I decided not to hiss and rake my nails down Gwendy's face.

"Come on! Let's go!" Dave ordered.

Never one to quit easily, he took off down the path.

Unfortunately, after 10 minutes of tripping around the dark, we still had no luck. It was late, and we were tired. No birds in the hand *or* in the bush, Dave and I grumbled our way back to bed. As we drifted to sleep that night, our dreams of seeing a kiwi bird would not be realized.

"Siiirrr, will you bring me a coffee?" I called to Dave from inside the van.

I was pushing my luck.

"I will if you show me your tits," he sing-sang in return.

He pushed his luck right back.

"Are you sure? They're moldy," I cracked.

"Oh dear. Why don't I just bring you a coffee then?"

"Thank you. You're such a gentleman."

Believe it or not, my breasts weren't actually covered in fungus. They were a little sticky at worst. It would be fair to say that, as the weeks turned into months on the road, our self-care relaxed. Dave, who preferred his haircuts with clippers, grew wild, gray, springing curls that I loved, and he wore his five o'clock shadow at any time of day. Meanwhile, I selected fashions that transitioned well from day to evening—to bed to morning—to day to evening again. In other words, we began to look like vagrants.

As we grew comfortable in New Zealand, I felt like we got a good sense of the place and the people. It was impossible to characterize the entire population of a country. For example, not all Americans wore plus-size blue jeans to church, but many did. Not all Brits wore jumpers or apologized on the

Tube. But it happened frequently. As we explored New Zealand, I began to notice a few trends among Kiwis.

New Zealanders weren't shy. Inquisitive and chatty, we often found ourselves drawn into conversations at grocery stores or in cafés. In general, locals seemed to want to hear our story and make conversation. I especially enjoyed the down-to-earth, confident women we met, who seemed to know what they thought and say what they meant.

Folks were outdoorsy. In a country that offered mountains, beaches, rivers, and lakes, it was entirely possible to have a three-sport day. An overwhelming number of young adults we came across had university degrees in Outdoor Education, and we encountered several school groups and retirees on the trails. It was possible that we met such athletic people because we were outside ourselves, but even the bigger cities like Auckland, Wellington, Christchurch, and Dunedin seemed full of people being active outside.

In 2018, to my delight, Kiwi men wore shorty shorts. Unlike the men from home who had been wearing long, baggy shorts for decades, the men of New Zealand wore fitted, pocketed shorts that came to mid-thigh or higher. It reminded me of the American 1970s, and I begged my husband, a man on the shorter side, to get a few pairs to show off his stocky pins. The shorty shorts would have looked great on him, but the macho man wouldn't budge.

Also, that year the women were into big, bushy eyebrows. Being blond myself, I'd long been a fan of eyelash and eyebrow tinting. Had I been in the habit of grooming myself in New Zealand, I would have been easily able to get those beauty treatments. However, in my opinion, the eyebrow trend had gone a little too far. Women in New Zealand, and all over the Western world, had taken to wearing great shaggy black caterpillars on their faces just above their eyes.

The southern portion of New Zealand's West Coast was possibly the most beautiful in the entire country. Home to two major parks, the Fjordlands

National Park and Mt. Aspiring National Park, hikers were humbled by snow-capped peaks, glittering fjords, raging rivers, thundering waterfalls, mirror lakes, golden tussocks and sheer, ice-carved valleys. Unlike the other six Great Walks, which were scattered around the country to highlight its diversity, the Kepler, Routeburn, and Milford Tracks were set together in this mountain paradise. Referred to as "The Walking Capital of the World," the Fjordlands were one of the most breathtaking places I'd ever stepped foot.

We met up with Gwen in Te Anau, the town we used as our hub for these three missions. Because the Fjordlands typically received over 200 days of rain per year, we prepared ourselves to be wet, something my British family took in stride. With a cyclone approaching to the north, the weather didn't disappoint.

Great Walk 7 – Kepler

"From the beech-forested shorelines of lakes Te Anau and Manapouri, to tussock-covered ridgelines and spectacular alpine vistas, the Kepler Track is an incredible wilderness adventure above the clouds."

We took four days and three nights to complete this 60-km (37-m) tramp. Scattered showers teased us all four days.

My parents never had much difficulty choosing a favorite kid. It was a title that changed often, and my older sister Julie and I took turns being "the Golden Child." It seemed to depend on who had been the sweetest or had done my parents a favor most recently; however, more often than not, the Golden Child crown was awarded to our family dog, our cocker spaniel brother named Benjamin. He lived to be 15. My sister and I were never upset when Ben won the title. We all agreed that our beautiful boy deserved it.

Unlike my parents with their children, it was difficult for me to pick a favorite Great Walk. Once people heard our story, I was inevitably asked to name the best hike. The winner switched around in my mind as we progressed, especially after those last three Great Walks in the Fjordlands. However, if pressed, I often returned to the Kepler, as my sweet Benjamin of the bunch.

I loved the Kepler for more than its major breathtaking view, which was stunning yet unpretentious. It charmingly forwent the bravado of its Fjordland siblings and had smaller crowds because of it. What made this hike my favorite was the wind! A storm, still too far away to be dangerous, was blowing in. Hiking along the Day Two ridgeline, through whipping, gale-force winds, I felt like a witch! I was filled with a sort of summoning joy, my hair wild, as I drank in the elements. Surrounded by that electrifying breeze on the Kepler, I felt so alive.

To take it down a notch, pragmatically, I also liked that the Kepler was a circular hike. It was one of only three Great Walks that actually returned to its origin, while the others required us to hire expensive land or water shuttles to get back to our van. Seeing as we were already spending a bundle on the huts, the added cost and hassle of transport irked. We were watching our money closely. Plus, as a person traveling the world on a year off, I needed *something* to complain about.

Just as Benjamin had hated the squirrels in our backyard, our Luxmore Hut ranger Mark was bloodthirsty for stoats.

"Behold! New Zealand's Bird Enemy Number One," Mark announced dramatically, and with a little trouble, whipped out a taxidermied stoat from his trouser pocket.

It was a small, weaselly-looking animal that I'd never heard of before.

"Did he say stouts?" I whispered to Dave as Mark talked.

What could delicious dark beer possibly have to do with this creature?

"'Stoats' not 'stouts.' We have them in England," he whispered back.

I shrugged and refocused.

A passionate bird conservationist, Mark certainly knew his facts. He launched into a compelling diatribe, listing all the reasons we should loathe these nasty bird-murderers. He enumerated the following points:

- First, stoats did not simply feed on birds and eggs; they killed for pleasure. Cameras had captured stoats decimating birds' nests, killing the birds and their babies inside, without eating the bodies or the eggs.

- Second, stoats could climb trees and swim almost 2 km (1.25 m). This meant that even the birds on isolated islands weren't protected from invasion.

- Third, stoats had nasty ways of reproducing. Males mated with multiple partners, forcing most of the females. It was no surprise to learn that they did not help the females raise the young.

- In turn, during a lonely pregnancy that could yield up to 12 kits, the females were able to utilize "delayed implantation." This meant they could delay the birth of their offspring until periods of safety when food, like birds and their eggs, was plentiful.

- Most disturbing of all, the male stoats invaded stoat dens and forced themselves on baby female kits. So, young females were often pregnant before they even left their mothers.

By the end of Mark's speech, I was seeing red. His talk put me into a crazed Berserker's rage. If he had handed me a basket full of live stoats, I swear I would have rung their wiry necks, one right after the next, and slung their bodies into a riotous crowd of chanting hut-mates. *Kill the Beasts! Kill the Beasts!* Thankfully, that wouldn't be necessary.

Mark showcased a model of the stoat traps that lined all the Great Walk trails, especially in the Fjordlands. Long, thin, double-ended wooden boxes, the traps were baited with a chicken egg or peanut butter. Each trap could kill two stoats at a time, and, based on the resurging bird population, it was clear that these traps were helping.

Mark had been inspired by a colleague, a Department of Conservation Ranger named Evan, who manned the Routeburn Track. Smith's Upper Hollyford Restoration Project was making a big difference for birds in New Zealand, and the trapping technique had spread to other Great Walks. Passionate hut rangers all over New Zealand, like Sunny, Aroha, Mark, and Evan, were doing their part to educate tourists and preserve their country's beautiful, diverse ecosystems.

My golden boy Benjamin would have approved.

With four days between each Fjordland hike, Dave and I passed the time in Te Anau by bickering. After all, we'd been living together in Van Halen for almost four months.

"Aaaaah Choo!" I splat.

"Bless you," Dave consoled.

"Paaaaah Chyoo!" I sneezed again.

"Bless you," Dave offered.

"Come on, Sir. Could you please just stop it with the 'Bless you-s.'"

"I beg your pardon, Madam?…No, I won't! It's the polite thing to do."

I'd offended his British sensibilities, yet again in life.

"Sir, it's exhausting. I'm already irritated that I've sneezed multiple times, and then you make me follow each one up with gratitude. Spare me the mother-luvin' pleasantries." (I didn't say "mother-luvin'").

Believe it or not, I didn't grow up at the base of Tina Turner's Thunderdome (from the 1985 Mad Max film by George Miller and George Ogilvie). I knew society had niceties for good reason, and I'd even learned to play along in public. With my own husband, however, these types of social delicacies seemed unnecessary. We were married. Couldn't we just, you know, assume good will?

Just then, Gwen entered the room. She took one look at us, froze, and slowly reversed back out the door.

"Can I just say 'ta' instead?" I asked a few minutes later.

Dave often used this British equivalent for a quick 'thanks,' and I appreciated its efficiency.

"Sure, that would be fine," Dave smiled, encouraged by my progress.

"Can I scream '*TA!*' in your face?" I asked.

"Oh, Madam!" Dave groaned.

In the end, we compromised. We agreed to shoot air pistols at each other after each of my many sneezes.

Great Walk 8 – Routeburn

"The Routeburn Track is the ultimate alpine adventure, taking you through ice-carved valleys and below the majestic peaks of the Southern Alps/Kā Tiritiri o te Moana.... Weaving through meadows, reflective tarns, and alpine gardens, you'll be rewarded with spectacular vistas over vast mountain ranges and valleys."

With the cyclone at its closest to the north, we were prepared for torrential rains and windstorms on the four-day, three-night, 32-km (20-m) trail. Instead, we endured the cold and scattered showers to tramp beneath mountains dusted with powdered sugar.

Up to that point, we were only aware of one kind of New Zealand hiking experience—trips for independent walkers. Self-guided and laden with our own gear, we preferred the challenge and reward of doing it ourselves. On the Routeburn Track, however, we met those who had gone for the luxury option: Guided Walks.

Our first clue that there was another way of hiking the Great Walks came as we approached the first hut. It looked like an enormous, fancy hotel. Through one window, I spied a king-sized bed with crisp white sheets. Around the corner, a wall of windows showcased a restaurant and bar.

My family was not impressed.

"Bloody hell! Did we take a wrong turn?" Dave looked around, confused.

"How ridiculous! This certainly wasn't in the brochure," Gwen agreed with disdain.

I shook my head in disgusted support, but a secret part of me thought, *Oooh, la, la!*

As we continued along a wooden deck, we soon came to a sign that pointed to "Routeburn Falls *Lodge*" on the left. "Routeburn Falls *Hut,*" our accommodation, was down to the right. It was concealed behind shrubbery, beneath the ridgeline. In this way, we supposed the rich people wouldn't have to see us, or worse—smell us.

"I guess we're around back in the servant quarters. We wouldn't want to upset the 'Fancy Trampers,'" Dave joked.

Later, we would learn that a private guided walking experience was available on the Routeburn and Milford tracks, the crème de la crème of all the Great Walks. For roughly $1,500 a pop, almost four times what we'd paid for the hut experience, luxury walkers could expect hot showers, clean sheets, three gourmet meals a day, snacks, alcohol, and baggage transport. Essentially, Fancy Trampers could still enjoy the same gorgeous walks, but without all the grunt or the funk. The poor bastards missed the whole point.

To be fair, I recognized that, in addition to rich city slickers, a guided walking experience might be a great option for elderly people, for someone with a disability, or for those with other health-related issues. My dodgy knees, for example, would have been much happier without the heavy backpack so, if it weren't for the cost, I could see the appeal in having one's bag transported. (By the way, my knee continued to hold up. It was tender so I was gentle, but I was no longer hiking in constant fear that it would snag at any point.) Alas, I was still too young, healthy, and miserly for the luxury hiking option.

Actually, the Routeburn Falls *Hut* was one of the nicest of all the Great Walks huts. With 48 single bunks, rather than those long shared multi-bunks, we each had our own space. Plus there were indoor flush toilets and a deck that peered into mountains. It, and the huts that followed, were part of a beautiful setting.

That first night, the hut ranger warned us about wildlife. Mischievous, infamous mountain thugs, parrots called keas, took delight in destroying tourists' gear. The ranger suggested bringing our items inside overnight, and also tying our boots together on the hooks outside since keas could carry away one boot but not two.

Also, we were encouraged to keep the bathroom doors closed. Evidently, a woman once locked herself in the toilet with a possum. When it brushed against her leg, she, of course, screamed! In the ensuing panic, she dropped her head torch. Locked inside together in the dark, the two woke up the entire hut.

Appropriately cautioned, we stayed mindful of the animals at night. I doubted that the luxury hikers in their safe, cozy lodge shared our wildlife concerns. Their choice baffled me. Honestly, who wouldn't want to poop with a possum?

As the days unfolded, we missed the worst of the forecasted weather. Instead of hammering rains and winds, we leapfrogged through scattered showers. Low clouds teased us with glimpses of mountaintops and fjords, but I suspected they concealed much of the legendary view. I wasn't too bothered because overall we'd had incredible luck with the weather in New Zealand, and the peeks we got on the Routeburn were mind-blowing. Out in the biting wind and cold, on one of the world's best hikes, Mother Nature reminded me how good it was to be healthy, alive, and outside.

And yet, of all our Great Walks, I would end up wishing for another crack at The Routeburn due to the clouds. I told myself that I would return one day when I was in my 70s. And, when I came back as a bionic little old lady, I'd be ready to embrace the whole experience as a Fancy Tramper.

With that fickle cruelty of vacation time, somehow suddenly, it was late February and time for our final Great Walk. We had saved New Zealand's most popular hike, the legendary tramp to Milford Sound, for last.

Great Walk 9 – Milford Track

"Experience the 'finest walk in the world' as you retrace the steps of early explorers on the world-renowned Milford Track. Take a journey along valleys carved by glaciers, wander through ancient rainforests, and admire cascading waterfalls."

Once rich with the Māori's treasured greenstone, or jade-like stones, the Milford Track had a rich native and visitor history, hosting vacationers since 1901. Over four days and three nights, we hiked 54 km (33.5 m) to complete the most famous of all Great Walks. We experienced a full range of weather, including two sunny days, a one-day deluge, and a pleasant, cloudy finish.

I looked around the ferry as we rumbled across the water to the start of our tramp.

Wow! Every person in here signed up for this hike almost a year ago, I thought to myself.

The Milford hike consistently sold out for the entire Great Walks season in less than a week, so at least one member from every group on our ferry had hustled to get their party a spot.

On a one-way hike that only allowed 40 freedom trampers each day, it was a mixed bag of incredibly prepared, determined walkers. On that first day, I affectionately noted 14 middle-aged South Koreans, not only because their big group could *not* be missed, but also because I'd lived in South Korea for a year. I also clocked the other Americans, four loud talkers, semi-retired folks whose company I would end up enjoying. As the days unfolded, I came to realize our numbers included an Australian couple with their grown daughter, and two married pairs of Kiwi-Russians, four single young men who would end up bonding together, and several others from various countries. We came from all over the world.

When we unloaded from the ferry, each group took a few minutes to situate themselves and most took a group picture at the starting sign. I offered to take the South Koreans' photo, and delighted them with the Korean I remembered from the 10 months I had lived there, 10 years earlier.

"Hanna, Dul, Set," I counted up before snapping their photo.

They smiled, laughed, and seemed to appreciate my gesture. If they found that impressive, I still remembered how to say: "No onions, please," "toilet," "ready, let's go!" "booger," and "diarrhea" in Korean. I'd have four days to see if I could work it all into other conversations.

Dave, Gwen, and I let all the other groups go ahead. We weren't in any hurry to get to the hut. It was a beautiful day, too, so we waited to bring up the rear.

Actually, we were very lucky with the forecast. In the country's rainiest region, we would have clear sunny skies those first two days. The locals had told us that rain on the Milford was always good because it boosted the waterfalls. However, I suspected they just said that to make tourists feel better about having crummy, cloudy weather on an experience that people had looked forward to for almost a year.

That first day, as we walked through a lush valley with steep granite cliffs on each side, we did see several long trickling waterfalls, high up on the rock faces. Sure, they would have been more impressive in the rain, but they were still lovely. As a hiker who struggled with Wet Cat Syndrome, I was perfectly okay with thin waterfalls and blue skies.

The pinnacle of the tramp would occur on Day Three when we were scheduled to climb up and over Mackinnon Pass. At 1,140 m (3,740 ft), it was the highest point of the hike, and on clear days, afforded a stunning view down into the renowned Milford Sound. Unfortunately, torrential rain was forecasted for that day.

The Terminator Siblings were thinking alike. That first night, at dinner in the hut, Dave laid out the plan:

"Let's push hard tomorrow and continue up to the pass," he suggested.

"Absolutely!" Gwen seconded. "It's our only chance for the view."

They both turned to me, and not for approval. Dave and Gwen would hate to go without me, but it was clear they would climb it regardless. The real question was if I would go. I weighed my options.

Climbing up to the Mackinnon Pass and back down to the hut would make for a long, 10- to 12-hour hiking day. I did worry about my gimpy knee, but I didn't want to be left behind or to miss the spectacular landscape. Plus, it was our last Great Walk. In the big picture, I figured, it didn't matter if my knee melted or ground down to a fine powder, as long as I could drag my carcass across the finish line. On this once-in-a-lifetime experience, in unusually nice weather, how could I not try for the top?

"Okay, I'm in."

The next morning we got up early, leaving a full hut behind us. For the first half of the gorgeous day, we continued along the waterfall valley, over boardwalks and wetlands, and up a gradual climb to Mintaro Hut, our stop for the night. There we dropped our heavy packs, ate a quick lunch, and continued up the mountain.

Ascending was never a problem for me. It took us almost three hours to reach the top of MacKinnon Pass, but it was worth every step. With crisp, clear, windless skies, the views were outstanding. Surrounded by glacial mountains, time for me stopped that afternoon. We peered down into two rich valleys—our past and future.

Dave brought the camp stove to make tea, and Gwen brought brownies. We celebrated on the summit that magical afternoon. We stayed a couple of hours, alone at the highpoint of the Milford Track. On a clear, sunny day, we had the best view of the 'finest walk in the world,' *all to ourselves.*

You better believe it was 'sweet as.'

The two-and-a-half hour descent back to Mintaro Hut was tedious, but blurred. Going down, my knee grew more and more tender, but nothing too terrible yet. We passed four others, on their way up as we headed back down. I was surprised by how few of our trail-mates made the ascent that day.

I was so glad we'd pushed to make the most of it.

The next day we woke to torrential rain. It lasted all day. A slog, we climbed up and over Mackinnon Pass, not pausing for a view because, in a giant rain cloud, there wasn't one. Plus, it was windy, wet, and cold, and we were eager to get out of the elements. I felt bad for most of my hut-mates, who had no idea what they'd missed. On the plus side, I supposed, the waterfalls were spectacular.

Doubling up the second day hadn't been free. For the last two days of the Milford tramp, my left knee grew to be intensely painful, much more than my normal peppermint pain. However, unlike my injury on the Abel Tasman, I was able to finish the hike. I managed it with four Advil, three times a day, for the final two days. Basically, I snacked on painkillers as if they were 'scroggin,' my own special version of New Zealand trail mix.

Loaded up with drugs, I hobbled to the finish line. To my mortification, Gwen and Dave walked patiently behind, witnessing every horrible, painful step. For weeks afterward, my knees, especially the left, would feel like loose molars—sore and shifty.

Along the way, I thought to myself, *Huh. This seems a lot like that 'femoral patella syndrome' the doctor described.* It was probably for the best that I hadn't tackled the physician. She had been right. Even though I hadn't lashed out at the time, I beamed a little apology to Dr. Fart Breath.

With enough rest between hikes I would heal.

"Cheers. Here's to finishing all nine!" Dave congratulated us all.

He held up his pint.

"Cheers," Gwen and I rejoined with lackluster.

"What is it?" Dave asked, confused by our underwhelmed reactions.

"Well, I didn't do all nine hikes," Gwen explained. "I only did five of the Great Walks. So congratulations to *you* both. That's a wonderful achievement!"

Gwen hadn't completed all nine walks only because it wasn't a goal she had set for herself. Instead, she'd fallen in love with high mountain passes and backcountry huts. In places like Gertrude Saddle, Rob Roy Glacier, Mount Cook and Mount Aspiring, Gwen thrived where she was more truly challenged, the more difficult hikes high above the treeline.

"Actually, I didn't do all nine either," I conceded. "With my knee injury on the Abel Tasman, I only did eight-and-a-half."

"Oh, don't be ridiculous," Gwen burst out.

"Ame, that's silly. Of course you did," Dave agreed.

The two argued that I'd essentially done all nine hikes. It was close enough. In the end, who would know that I hadn't actually finished the Abel Tasman?

I would.

"I'm serious, you guys," I said. "If my knee recovers in time, I need to go back and try again."

After all, a person can't do eight-and-a-half Great Walks.

The next morning we said goodbye to Gwen, who was making her way back to England. The future uncertain, we weren't sure if it would be months or years before we'd next see her. We were sad to see her go. But, I was thankful for the serendipitous time we'd been able to share with Dave's sister in Africa and New Zealand during our midlife gap year.

After Dave and I completed the Milford, our last planned hike and the final bone in the skeleton of our schedule, we used our remaining five weeks in New Zealand, to flesh out any gaps and to revisit our favorite places. I rebooked reservations for the Abel Tasman Track, thankful that it hadn't sold out, for our penultimate week in NZ. I was unsure if my knee would be up for it when the time finally arrived.

In the meantime, we recuperated in the beautiful mountain town of Glenorchy. Fording rivers down dusty "unsealed" roads, we visited the village "Paradise" and the valley beyond. From there we drove along the Southern Scenic Route, checking out the south coast from west to east. We explored the Caitlyns and went on a yellow-eyed penguin safari. We passed through Dunedin, checked out the Moeraki Boulders, and headed north to the Steampunk Headquarters in Oamaru. We even made our way back to Murchison to take another kayaking course, further cementing our love for the sport.

Finally, with two weeks left in New Zealand, we returned to the Abel Tasman Track. Once there, we retraced our path to Cleopatra's Pool, just beyond the first hut.

"Well, here we are," I said to Dave. "I think this is about where we turned back."

"Indeed. That feels so long ago."

Two-and-a-half months had passed.

"Are you ready?" Dave asked, nodding at me with a smile.

"Let's do it," I replied and grabbed his hand.

With my partner at my side, I took the first stride into new territory. After that step, followed another. And then another.

Four days later, I finally accomplished what I'd set out to do: I'd finished all nine of New Zealand's Great Walks.

Well, technically, it was eight and two half-tramps.

A week later, on the outskirts of Christchurch, Dave and I were curled up in Halen for our final night in the van. Our travels through New Zealand had come to an end, and our year off was nearly finished. For the second time in our trip, I found myself holed up in the van, and contemplating growing older, my failing body, and the inescapable death of all living things.

I hugged into Dave. My husband was 14 years older, and I came from a family of women who lived into their 90s. I knew that futures were never certain, but even if our silver years went as well as they possibly could, chances were good that I would have to live 20 years without this man. My guts hurt to imagine it. I knew our time on Earth together was limited, but I also had no doubt that we would make the most of it.

Thank you for him. Thank you for our families. Thank you for all the friendship and love I've known. Thank you for this beautiful planet and my life on it. Amy is here.

I sent a signal into the universe.

GOODBYE

International Life, 2003–Present

Living internationally I've had to learn how to kiss my greetings and good-byes. With greasy cheeks pressed, I puff air into ears and wonder if I should add "the accompanying hug." It depends on the person and the circumstance so, inevitably, I get it wrong. I've accidentally snubbed Great Old Aunties with my cold wave yet generous smile. Equally, I've made out with bank manag-ers, pressing my breasts into their chests as their handshakes melt into the small of my back. I dread these stumbling moments. I never know what to do.

It affects my writing, too. Unfortunately, I find myself signing off with "xo-Amy." I can't seem to help it. Despite reading like a 5th grader's yearbook, it's a true reflection of what happens physically, especially with my British family, so I've adopted the closing in adulthood.

My overthinking makes things awkward. I'm more comfortable with hugs, or better yet *side-hugs*, and I would prefer to sign with something like "oo-Amy" or "O-Amy." However, I worry about this, too. Will my friends know what my "o" means? And if I capitalize them, sending big Os, will people think I'm sending orgasms?

Fifty-eight percent of my personal profits from

Sweet Astrid will be donated to causes close to my heart.

I'm keeping the rest.

42%

OOO,

Amy

June 1, 2020

Bryson City, North Carolina, USA

Acknowledgements

Deepest thanks to my midwives and beta-readers, Regina Landor, Sophie Manekuleh, and Cathie Turek. Your thoughtful remarks and attention to detail helped bring this book, an enormous life goal of mine, into being. Thanks for your friendship, honesty, and for sparing the rest of my readers loads of confusion, boredom, and offense. Or so we hope.

To my sister Julie Neal Wilson for getting all my jokes. This book wouldn't have happened without your encouragement, early feedback, and tech skills. You have always been, and you will always be, an essential part of my story.

To my parents for deep roots, unconditional love, and for teaching me how to laugh at myself.

To my family and friends in the book who trusted (or perhaps just tolerated) me to write about you. Thank you for the benefit of any doubts. Know that I love you guys, and remember—I'm watching.

To Jess Boerema, Janine Plunkett, and Jenny Lind. Thank you for making sure my Kiwi, South African, and German characters talked and cussed just right. It's all in the bladdy details.

To the Department of Conservation in New Zealand for their descriptions of the Nine Great Walks.

To Wikipedia for being a quick, go-to resource for a person like me and countless others.

To my readers. Thank you for your encouragment through the years and for your support with this project. I hope you enjoyed the book. If so, my ego and I would appreciate your efforts to promote *Sweet Astrid* on social media, with book reviews on websites like Amazon and Goodreads, and through word of mouth. Pass it on. Or not. I'm grateful, regardless.

Finally, to Dave. Sir, thank you for endless cups of tea and for the time and space to make this book happen. *What's next on the spreadsheet, my love?*